Canada and International Affairs

Series Editors
David Carment, NPSIA, Carleton University, Ottawa, ON, Canada
Philippe Lagassé, NPSIA, Carleton University, Ottawa, ON, Canada
Yiagadeesen Samy, NPSIA, Carleton University, Ottawa, ON, Canada

Palgrave's Canada and International Affairs is a timely and rigorous series for showcasing scholarship by Canadian scholars of international affairs and foreign scholars who study Canada's place in the world. The series will be of interest to students and academics studying and teaching Canadian foreign, security, development and economic policy. By focusing on policy matters, the series will be of use to policy makers in the public and private sectors who want access to rigorous, timely, informed and independent analysis. As the anchor, Canada Among Nations is the series' most recognisable annual contribution. In addition, the series showcases work by scholars from Canadian universities featuring structured analyses of Canadian foreign policy and international affairs. The series also features work by international scholars and practitioners working in key thematic areas that provides an international context against which Canada's performance can be compared and understood.

Thomas Juneau · Philippe Lagassé
Editors

Canadian Defence Policy in Theory and Practice, Volume 2

Second Edition

Editors
Thomas Juneau
Graduate School of Public
and International Affairs
University of Ottawa
Ottawa, ON, Canada

Philippe Lagassé
Norman Paterson School
of International Affairs
Carleton University
Ottawa, ON, Canada

ISSN 2523-7187 ISSN 2523-7195 (electronic)
Canada and International Affairs
ISBN 978-3-031-37541-5 ISBN 978-3-031-37542-2 (eBook)
https://doi.org/10.1007/978-3-031-37542-2

© The Editor(s) (if applicable) and The Author(s), under exclusive license to Springer Nature Switzerland AG 2020, 2023

This work is subject to copyright. All rights are solely and exclusively licensed by the Publisher, whether the whole or part of the material is concerned, specifically the rights of translation, reprinting, reuse of illustrations, recitation, broadcasting, reproduction on microfilms or in any other physical way, and transmission or information storage and retrieval, electronic adaptation, computer software, or by similar or dissimilar methodology now known or hereafter developed.
The use of general descriptive names, registered names, trademarks, service marks, etc. in this publication does not imply, even in the absence of a specific statement, that such names are exempt from the relevant protective laws and regulations and therefore free for general use.
The publisher, the authors, and the editors are safe to assume that the advice and information in this book are believed to be true and accurate at the date of publication. Neither the publisher nor the authors or the editors give a warranty, expressed or implied, with respect to the material contained herein or for any errors or omissions that may have been made. The publisher remains neutral with regard to jurisdictional claims in published maps and institutional affiliations.

Cover illustration: Contributor: Cameron Ballantyne-Smith/Alamy Stock Photo

This Palgrave Macmillan imprint is published by the registered company Springer Nature Switzerland AG
The registered company address is: Gewerbestrasse 11, 6330 Cham, Switzerland

Acknowledgements

This book is the second volume in what we hope will become a continuous series on Canadian defence policy. The first volume, published in 2019, offered 23 chapters on a wide range of topics, written by a broad range of academics and practitioners. This first book filled an important niche: there had not been a comprehensive book on Canadian defence policy published since the mid-1990s. It has since been widely circulated and read, in paper and electronic versions, in the Canadian Armed Forces, the Department of National Defence, elsewhere in government, in academia, and among other interested stakeholders. For this second volume, instead of a revised and updated edition, we chose to put together a smaller collection of chapters on topics that were not covered in the first volume.

We wish to thank the University of Ottawa's Centre for International Policy Studies (CIPS), which provided financial support for the preparation of this book. We also wish to thank Nabil Jaafari for his skilled assistance in preparing the manuscript.

We also wish to thank the three discussants who provided chapter authors with highly valuable feedback and comments during the workshop we organized in December 2022: Kerry Buck, a senior fellow with the Graduate School of Public and International Affairs at the University of Ottawa and a retired senior Canadian diplomat and ambassador to NATO; Charlotte Duval-Lantoine, the Ottawa operations manager and a fellow with the Canadian Global Affairs Institute; and Gordon Venner, a retired senior Canadian diplomat and associate deputy minister with the Department of National Defence.

We also wish to offer special thanks to the chapter authors, who agreed to take time out of their busy schedules to contribute to this collection. Special thanks go to Srdjan Vucetic, who co-edited the first volume with us, and will continue to manage this series.

Finally, we again thank Anca Pusca and Geetha Chockalingam from Palgrave for their indispensable support and assistance throughout this project.

Ottawa, Canada

Thomas Juneau
Philippe Lagassé

Contents

Introduction — 1
Thomas Juneau and Philippe Lagassé

Sexual Misconduct and the Crisis of Defence Culture — 9
Megan MacKenzie

Canadian Armed Forces Reconstitution: The Critical Role of Personnel Retention — 29
Irina Goldenberg and Nancy Otis

Climate Insecurity and Canadian Defence — 51
Wilfrid Greaves

NORAD Modernization: Past, Present and Future — 75
Andrea Charron and James Fergusson

Canada's Defence Policy Trade-Offs — 97
Stéfanie von Hlatky and Srdjan Vucetic

The Defence Budget — 113
Dave Perry

Defence Policy and Procurement Costs: The Case for Pessimism Bias   133
Philippe Lagassé

The Making of Defence Policy in Canada   151
Thomas Juneau and Vincent Rigby

LIST OF CONTRIBUTORS

Andrea Charron Department of Political Studies, University of Manitoba, Winnipeg, MB, Canada

James Fergusson Department of Political Studies, University of Manitoba, Winnipeg, MB, Canada

Irina Goldenberg Ottawa, ON, Canada

Wilfrid Greaves Department of Political Science, University of Victoria, Victoria, BC, Canada

Thomas Juneau Graduate School of Public and International Affairs, University of Ottawa, Ottawa, ON, Canada

Philippe Lagassé Norman Paterson School of International Affairs, Carleton University, Ottawa, ON, Canada

Megan MacKenzie Simon Fraser University, Vancouver, BC, Canada

Nancy Otis Ottawa, ON, Canada

Dave Perry Canadian Global Affairs Institute, Ottawa, ON, Canada

Vincent Rigby Max Bell School of Public Policy, McGill University, Montreal, QC, Canada

Stéfanie von Hlatky Department of Political Studies, Queen's University, Kingston, ON, Canada

Srdjan Vucetic Graduate School of Public and International Affairs, University of Ottawa, Ottawa, ON, Canada

Acronyms

ALCM	Air Launched Cruise Missile
BMEWS	Ballistic Missile Early Warning System
C2	Command and Control
CADIZ	Canada's Air Defence Identification Zone
CAF	Canadian Armed Forces
CANUS	Canada-United States
CASCOE	Climate and Security Centre of Excellence
CDS	Chief of the Defence Staff
CFACC	Combined Forces (Canada and US) Air Component Command
CFD	Chief of Force Development
CFDS	Canada First Defence Strategy
CFINTCOM	Canadian Forces Intelligence Command
CJOC	Canadian Joint Operations Command
CMAC	Court Martial Appeal Court of Canada
CSE	Communications Security Establishment
CSIS	Canadian Security Intelligence Service
DART	Disaster Assistance Response Team
DEES	Defence Energy and Environment Strategy
DND	Department of National Defence
DPS	Defence Policy Statement
eFP	enhanced Forward Presence
FOL	Forward Operating Location
GAC	Global Affairs Canada
GDP	Gross Domestic Product
GHG	Greenhouse Gas Emissions

GIUK	Greenland-Iceland-United Kingdom
GTFAD	Global Trends, Foreign Affairs, and Defence
INF	Intermediate Nuclear Forces
ISAF	International Security Assistance Force
ISED	Innovation, Science and Economic Development Canada
ITB	Industrial and Technical Benefit
ITW/AA	Integrated Tactical Warning/Attack Assessment
JADC2	Joint All Domain Command and Control
LAV	Light Armoured Vehicle
MAD	Mutual Assured Destruction
MND	Minister of National Defence
MSV	Military Sexual Violence
MWSA	Military Work-Related Sexual Assault
NASS	Northern Approaches Surveillance System
NATO	North Atlantic Treaty Organization
NCA	National Command Authorities
NORAD	North American Aerospace Defence Command
NSS	National Safety and Security Operations
NWS	North Warning System
O&M	Operations and Maintenance
OTHR	Over-the-Horizon Radar
PBO	Parliamentary Budget Officer
PMO	Prime Minister's Office
PRC	People's Republic of China
PSPC	Public Services and Procurement Canada
PTSD	Post-Traumatic Stress Disorder
RCN	Royal Canadian Navy
SAR	Search and Rescue
SCC	Supreme Court of Canada
SecDef	Secretary of Defense
SSE	Strong, Secure, Engaged
SSMCAF	Sexual Misconduct in the Canadian Armed Forces
START	Strategic Arms Reduction Treaties
USNORTHCOM	US Northern Command

List of Figures

Sexual Misconduct and the Crisis of Defence Culture

Fig. 1   Canada defining scandals   16
Fig. 2   Zero tolerance statements found in media coverage of MSV
         in Canada   17

Canadian Armed Forces Reconstitution: The Critical Role of Personnel Retention

Fig. 1   Shortlist of factors related to retention   33

Canada's Defence Policy Trade-Offs

Fig. 1   Opportunities/constraints   103

The Defence Budget

Fig. 1   Data reflects total ministry spending, or estimated spending,
         on a cash basis. Public Accounts, Vol. 2 various years,
         Supplementary Estimates C, 2022/2023, Main Estimates
         2023/2024, and projected spending from Strong, Secure,
         Engaged, converted to $2023/2024 Billions by the author
         using DND's Economic Models (various years)   116

Fig. 2 Data reflects Vote 5 spending, or estimated spending, on a cash basis. Public Accounts, Vol. 2 various years, Supplementary Estimates C, 2022/2023, Main Estimates 2023/2024, and projected spending from Strong, Secure, Engaged provided to the author, converted to $2023/2024 billions by the author using DND's Economic Models (various years) 117

Fig. 3 SSE 20-year cash flow (*Sources* PBO, DND) 118

Defence Policy and Procurement Costs: The Case for Pessimism Bias

Fig. 1 The iron triangle 139

List of Tables

The Defence Budget

Table 1	Canadian defence spending by component ($2021/2022B)	119
Table 2	Budget 2021 defence measures ($ millions)	121
Table 3	Millions, accrual basis	123
Table 4	NORAD modernization investments (billions, accrual basis)	128

Introduction

Thomas Juneau and Philippe Lagassé

In 2019, we co-edited volume one of *Canadian Defence Policy in Theory and Practice* (along with our colleague Srdjan Vucetic), the first comprehensive book on Canada's defence policy in 25 years. The book covered a wide range of issues and included 23 chapters on military and defence topics such as demographics, relations with First Nations, the budget process, relations with the United States, emerging technologies, accountability, strategic culture, and the role of Parliament.

Much has happened in the realm of Canadian defence policy since 2019. The crisis of sexual misconduct in the Canadian Armed Forces (CAF), in particular, has focused renewed attention on a critical failure within the military, one that threatens the future viability of the armed

---

T. Juneau
Graduate School of Public and International Affairs, University of Ottawa, Ottawa, ON, Canada
e-mail: thomas.juneau@uottawa.ca

P. Lagassé (✉)
Norman Paterson School of International Affairs, Carleton University, Ottawa, ON, Canada
e-mail: philippe.lagasse@carleton.ca

© The Author(s), under exclusive license to Springer Nature Switzerland AG 2023
T. Juneau and P. Lagassé (eds.), *Canadian Defence Policy in Theory and Practice, Volume 2*, Canada and International Affairs, https://doi.org/10.1007/978-3-031-37542-2_1

forces if left unaddressed, as former Supreme Court Justice Louise Arbour noted in her May 2022 report. There is increasing awareness that climate change will have major repercussions in virtually every facet of CAF operations in coming decades. Russia's invasion of Ukraine has seemingly reinvigorated NATO and Canada's commitment to European security. As we write these words, the government is working on an update to its 2017 policy *Strong, Secure, Engaged* (SSE). The government has also committed to invest significantly in continental defence, pledging $36.8 billion to modernize the North American Aerospace Defence Command (NOARD). Several large-scale procurements are moving forward as well, such as the acquisition of the F-35 Joint Strike Fighter to replace the CF-18 Hornets and the selection of the Type 26 design for the Canadian Surface Combatant. The past four years have been, without a doubt, a time of important change and challenge for Canadian defence policy.

In this context, we believe that it is timely to publish a second volume of *Canadian Defence Policy in Theory and Practice*. This is not a revised and updated edition. Instead, we have identified eight important policy issues that have either significantly gained in salience since 2019 or that we did not cover in the first volume. This is therefore a shorter book. Our intent is, moreover, to publish a new volume every four years. Doing so will allow scholars and practitioners to keep pace with policy developments, recurring cultural and organizational challenges, and evolutions in the international and domestic security environment that surround Canadian defence affairs and the management and deployment of Canada's armed forces.

Key Trends

In the years since we published the first volume of *Canadian Defence Policy in Theory and Practice*, the CAF have faced a long overdue reckoning over sexual misconduct. The problem of sexual misconduct in the CAF had been documented before, leading to the publication of a report by former Supreme Court Justice Marie Deschamps in 2015. The Deschamps report highlighted that the CAF were riven by a sexualized culture that enabled and excused sexual misconduct across the ranks. The military justice system routinely failed to properly investigate sexual misconduct or prioritize victims. This finding was reinforced by a review of the military justice system conducted by former Supreme

Court Justice Morris Fish in 2021. Indeed, leading up to the publication of Fish's report, revelations that several senior CAF leaders had previously been the subject of allegations of sexual misconduct came to the fore. These included an allegation that the newly appointed Chief of the Defence Staff (CDS), Admiral Art McDonald, had acted inappropriately towards a subordinate earlier in his career. Although no charges were laid against Admiral McDonald, the government replaced him as CDS after he publicly requested that he be allowed to return to duty. Another general officer, Major-General Dany Fortin, was removed as the Public Health Agency of Canada's vice-president for logistics and operations (a position in which he helped manage the logistics of vaccine delivery during the pandemic) following an allegation of sexual misconduct during his time as an officer-cadet at the Royal Military College of Canada. Major-General Fortin was subsequently charged with sexual assault for events that occurred in 1988 and was later acquitted. He has since launched a suit against the government that could test the nature of the relationship between the executive and the armed forces. Charges were also laid against the Chief of Military Personnel and allegations made against other senior officers. Still other senior officers were held to have supported fellow officers and subordinates facing allegations of sexual assault. When combined with Deschamps' and Fish's findings that the military is unable to effectively address sexual misconduct, these high-profile examples highlighted the CAF's deep-seated cultural failures.

The case that most encapsulated the dysfunctions of the military justice system, the CAF's sexualized culture, and the refusal of civilian authorities to address the problem was that of General Jonathan Vance, Canada's longest serving CDS. Vance had maintained a relationship with a subordinate for many years, fathering a child with her. When an investigation was launched into the relationship, Vance had asked her to lie, leading to an obstruction of justice charge to which he later pled guilty. As well, Vance was accused of sending a sexually inappropriate email to another subordinate. Military police and departmental officials were aware of the allegations against Vance. Yet, as Vance himself intimated when an investigation was being considered, his rank at the top of the military chain of command made it nearly impossible to effectively look into his behaviour, let alone charge him under the military justice system. Addressing the allegations against Vance would have required ministerial intervention. To that end, the military ombudsman raised the issue with Harjit Sajjan, the defence minister at the time. Sajjan, however, refused to discuss the matter. Coupled with the failure of the government to implement the recommendations of the Deschamps report, the minister's refusal to examine the allegations against Vance showed that the CAF was not only facing a crisis of sexual misconduct but of civil-military relations as well. Looking ahead, the government's response to the Arbour report will demonstrate whether the civil-military crisis allows the crises of sexual misconduct and sexualized culture to endure.

Because of the extensive training, education, and socialization that CAF members require to meet the unique demands of military service, personnel recruitment and retention are among the CAF's top strategic priorities. Yet like other militaries, the CAF suffer from retention challenges as well as reduced intake and training capacity, notably as a result of its organizational culture crisis and the COVID-19 pandemic. The CAF's commitments to operations and international peace and security have further contributed to burnout and exhaustion, challenging CAF readiness and the military personnel system. Meanwhile, preventing attrition of trained personnel is getting harder in today's competitive job market. As a result, the CAF have undertaken the CAF Reconstitution initiative to return to 71,500 Regular Force and 30,000 Reserve Force members, as originally outlined in SSE. This initiative comprises several simultaneous strategic objectives, including modernizing recruitment, streamlining training and other personnel production requirements, and increasing diversity, with a fundamental focus on personnel retention.

One of the most important topics that we did not directly address in the first volume is that of climate change and its impact on the military. We did partially deal with it in the chapter on the Arctic by Whitney Lackenbauer and Adam Lajeunesse, but the issue has become more prominent since. Climate change will have direct impacts on national security; it will, for example, exacerbate conflicts and accelerate and transform migratory patterns. This might increase demands on CAF expeditionary operations. At the same time, climate change will lead to the intensification of a trend we are already witnessing: growing demands on domestic operations, notably in response to natural disasters such as floods and forest fires. Balancing these competing priorities will be increasingly complex. In addition, climate change will force difficult and costly adjustments on the CAF, as they seek to green their operations by reducing their dependency on fossil fuels.

Relations with the United States, Canada's most important defence partner, have remained at the forefront of defence policy debates. SSE, however, left important questions unanswered, especially on issues of continental defence. In spring of 2022, defence minister Anita Anand announced that a decision had been made about NORAD modernization, the so-called missing chapter of SSE. As part of Canada's $38.6 billion investment to modernize NORAD, the government has promised to invest in command and control, communications, satellites, infrastructure in the north, air-to-air refuelling, and research and development. This pledge was reiterated when American President Joe Biden made his first visit to Ottawa in March 2023. Looking forward, Canada—in general, and specifically the Department of National Defence (DND) and the CAF—will have to adapt to growing uncertainty surrounding the future of American foreign and defence policy. Canada's defence relations with the United States survived the Trump years largely unscathed. But what if Donald Trump, or a like-minded Republican, wins the presidency in November 2024? How would bilateral relations be affected by a return to the unpredictability, unilateralism, and dismissiveness towards international norms and institutions that would follow?

Russia's invasion of Ukraine in February 2022 has also had dramatic consequences for Canada's defence policy. The invasion has seemingly reinvigorated NATO, a traditional pillar of Canada's defence policy whose future had seemed less certain after the shock of four years of the Trump administration. The invasion and Ottawa's response raise important questions about the future of Canada's international defence priorities. For years, successive governments, and virtually all analysts, have argued that the rise of the Indo-Pacific makes it a growing priority for Canada and its allies. Ottawa, however, has mostly failed to follow up on the defence front, as it has invested few additional resources in the region. As Canada ramps up its presence in Eastern Europe in response to Russia's invasion of Ukraine, a commitment that is likely to last for several years, how will its stated objectives to also ramp up its presence in the Indo-Pacific be impacted? And, caught in the middle between the Indo-Pacific and Europe, can Canada continue to afford to commit to several missions in the Middle East?

Defence procurement remains an ongoing challenge as well, despite the progress made on high-profile acquisitions such as fighter aircraft and warships. SSE outlined a significant reinvestment in the CAF, with a capital programme totalling more than $100 billion. This represented a major recapitalization effort, one that equalled the modernization of the military of the 1970s and 1980s. While the 2017 defence policy provided guidance and funds to undertake this regeneration of the armed forces, long-standing procurement challenges have remained stubbornly difficult to overcome. Above all, the defence department and the armed forces still lack the personnel to effectively manage projects and move them effectively through Canada's complex and demanding procurement system. In addition, the costing attached to SSE for capital projects proved optimistic in many cases. Several important acquisitions proved to be underfunded when they progressed through options analysis and definition. While the introduction of accrual accounting and better management of contingency funds have improved the procurement process and allowed projects to move forward, many others have had to wait for additional funding or been forced to reduce their original scope to stay within budget. This will inevitably mean that some of the future capabilities envisaged by SSE will be diluted or delayed.

The COVID-19 pandemic and its wider effects have exacerbated these procurement challenges. Inflation and supply chain interruptions have eroded the purchasing power of an already underfunded capital programme. Since defence sector inflation was already much higher than average prior to the pandemic, the long-term effects of the post-pandemic inflationary situation will have a corrosive effect on the government's ability to acquire the capabilities that are required to fulfil Canada's defence policy objectives. The pandemic further contributed to personnel shortages within the CAF and will likely impact industries that provide essential support, maintenance, and training to the military. In this context, every delay—be it due to improper costing, scope changes, contract negotiations, or Treasury Board approvals—will lead to a less capable CAF. More money, moreover, will not easily alleviate these inflationary and budgetary pressures. The difficulty DND/CAF have in moving projects forward and spending the funds that have been allocated will persist. Reforms that could accelerate the procurement process without sacrificing due diligence, increasing risks, or undermining Canadian industry, furthermore, remain necessary but frustratingly elusive. While the announcement of new initiatives such as NORAD modernization is good news for the defence of Canada and Canadian alliances, it is also important to recognize that the procurement system is already having difficulty delivering the capital programme outlined in SSE.

Finally, as the domestic and international security environments in which the CAF operate evolve, the issue of the governance of defence policymaking also emerges. Are DND and the CAF—and, more broadly, the government of Canada—well equipped to deal with recent and future developments in the defence realm? The intensification of great power competition will likely lead to growing calls from allies for the CAF to participate in missions and operations abroad. At the same time, pressures will mount on the CAF to conduct more domestic operations. The COVID-19 pandemic, in particular, saw the CAF involved in the distribution of vaccines across Canada and in providing personnel to support overwhelmed long-term care facilities. These developments will call on the DND and the CAF to adjust how defence policy is developed and implemented. The growing demands for domestic operations, for example, will steer DND/CAF to develop new relationships and to deepen existing ones with a range of domestic actors in provincial and municipal governments as well as in the private sector and civil society.

Plan of the Book

We address these themes in this second volume of *Canadian Defence Policy in Theory and Practice*. In her chapter "Sexual Misconduct and the Crisis of Defence Culture", Megan MacKenzie analyzes the crisis of defence culture in the CAF and looks at what the Forces have done to tackle sexual misconduct within the ranks. In their chapter "Canadian Armed Forces Reconstitution: The Critical Role of Personnel Retention", Irina Goldenberg and Nancy Otis discuss the issue of personnel retention within the CAF and explain how the CAF is seeking to reconstitute itself. In his chapter "Climate Insecurity and Canadian Defence", Will Greaves examines the impact that climate change has on Canadian defence. Andrea Charron and Jim Fergusson then explain in their chapter "NORAD Modernization: Past, Present, and Future" the challenges that Canada faces in pursuing the modernization of NORAD. In their chapter "Canada's Defence Policy Trade-offs", Stéfanie von Hlatky and Srdjan Vucetic examine the trade-offs that Canada's commitment to supporting Ukraine will imply for its defence policy. David Perry follows in his chapter "The Defence Budget" with an overview of defence spending since SSE was released in 2017. In his chapter "Defence Policy and Procurement Costs: The Case for Pessimism Bias", Philippe Lagassé examines how misalignments between defence policy and capital budgets exacerbate procurement challenges in Canada. Finally, in their chapter "The Making of Defence Policy in Canada", Thomas Juneau and Vincent Rigby explain the machinery of the defence policymaking process in Canada.

Sexual Misconduct and the Crisis of Defence Culture

Megan MacKenzie

Available data and research show that sexual violence committed by service members against fellow service members—or military sexual violence (MSV)—is pervasive and rampant in most western militaries. For example, in Australia, female service members have a one in four chance of being harassed or assaulted over the course of their career.[1] Between 2016 and 2018, the US military saw a 38% increase in cases of sexual assault,[2] and in July 2019, the Canadian government announced that it would pay nearly CAD 1 billion to members of the military who were part of a class action lawsuit claiming systemic and widespread sexual misconduct in the Canadian Armed Forces.[3] Nearly 19,000 Canadian Armed Forces and defence personnel submitted claims as part of this class action lawsuit.[4] There is strong evidence that available data on MSV is merely the tip of the iceberg; research from several countries indicates that over 80% of victims do not report their assault.[5]

Military sexual violence affects victims deeply and can have complex and long-term impacts on the health and well-being of victims. Sexual

M. MacKenzie (✉)
Simon Fraser University, Vancouver, BC, Canada
e-mail: m_mackenzie@sfu.ca

violence is associated with pregnancy and gynaecological complications, sexually transmitted diseases, an increased risk of suicide and suicide ideation, post-traumatic stress, career interruption, and social ostracization. Besides the significant and deep impacts of this violence on individuals, there are massive institutional and public costs associated with MSV. While it might seem insensitive to talk about financial costs related to MSV, national militaries spend millions of dollars every year to settle sexual abuse claims. Between 2017 and 2020 Australia spent $50 million on sexual abuse claims.[6] Although it is difficult to secure an accurate figure, the estimated costs of addressing the health impacts of sexual assault on US veterans is $872 million.[7] In addition to the costs of settling claims, there are a number of direct and indirect 'costs' associated with MSV, including the costs associated with investigations, training, victim support, recruitment to replace service members, and time off work due to injury, mental health, or for disciplinary measures.

Despite evidence that it is a regular and predictable problem across many national militaries, MSV has not been brought into the fold of global efforts to address, understand, and reduce sexual violence. For example, the United Nations' *Women, Peace and Security Agenda* aims to reduce international gender-based violence and exploitation; and variations of the #MeToo and #TimesUp movements have raised awareness about sexual harassment and abuse in a number of industries. However, these efforts have largely overlooked sexual violence that occurs *within* national militaries.[8] In addition, the established body of academic literature theorizing and examining sexual violence, rape culture, and rape myths is largely focused on civilians, and in the context of MSV, is primarily centred on case studies, 'scandals,' and limited empirical data.

While global efforts to address sexual violence and understand rape culture have failed to address MSV, national efforts to address MSV have also floundered. In Canada, despite increased attention to MSV, dedicated resources and public commitments by a series of Canadian governments and defence leaders, there is no evidence that rates of MSV are declining. For at least the last 30 years most western national defence forces, including the Canadian Armed Forces, (CAF) have been caught in a cycle of high-profile cases of MSV followed by sober declarations by military and government leaders of 'zero tolerance' and commitment to change. Moreover, not only is the CAF caught in a cycle of scandal and recommitment when it comes to MSV, in the past few years the CAF has been rocked as several senior military leaders—including two Chiefs of the Defence Staff—face allegations of MSV.

In short, MSV is a global problem, with long-reaching impacts and has sparked a national crisis of confidence in the Canadian Armed Forces. This chapter puts the current Canadian 'crisis' moment in both a broader national and international context. There are two main goals in the chapter. The first is to show a pattern of increased media attention, commitment to zero tolerance, and then relative inaction related to MSV. Media attention to MSV ebbs and flows dramatically and often centres on cases that are considered particularly salacious or extraordinary. These high-profile cases, or scandals, are politically important as they often set the tone for conversations for decades to come. Analysing this pattern is essential in understanding if and how increased media and national attention translates into significant and impactful policy changes with regard to MSV. This analysis also helps support an argument that the CAF and government response has often been prompted by scandal and the consistency with which the CAF has claimed 'zero tolerance' over the past three decades. A second goal of the chapter is to argue that MSV is a symptom of a wider dysfunctional military culture that requires radical change, led by the Canadian government. In doing so, this chapter helps answer key questions related to the current 'crisis' moment in Canada, including: is this a 'watershed' moment that will evoke real and lasting change?; what role do 'zero tolerance' statements and formal reviews play in addressing MSV?; and, what role does the media play in agenda setting and inspiring policy responses when it comes to MSV?

This chapter begins with a discussion of how MSV is defined and how data on MSV is collected in the CAF. This is followed by a brief overview of key scandals and defining moments related to MSV in the CAF, including high-profile cases and major policy changes. This forms the foundation for the central argument of the chapter, which relates to the pattern of zero tolerance statements and relative inaction by the CAF when it comes to MSV.

Defining and Collecting Data on MSV

In order to understand the scope of the problem of MSV, it is important to start with how MSV is defined and how data on the problem is collected. There is no cross-nationally accepted definition of MSV, which makes it challenging to compare data or discuss the issue beyond national contexts. The types of terms that most national militaries use in reference to sexual violence are constantly changing, yet often remain distinct from the terminology used to describe civilian sexual violence. Adding further confusion, researchers use a variety of terms and focus on different aspects of assault or harassment when collecting data or conducting research on MSV. I use the term MSV because it captures the range of sexual assault and violence activities and moves away from treating different forms of violence separately or as a hierarchy based on perceived impact to the victim.

The CAF use the term 'sexual misconduct' and include sexual misconduct as a sub-category of "improper conduct." The CAF refer to a "spectrum" of behaviours, or "the range of attitudes, beliefs, and actions that contribute to a toxic work environment" in their definitions.[9] The CAF define sexual misconduct as "conduct of a sexual nature that can cause or causes harm to others" and includes a listing of activities that constitute sexual misconduct, from jokes to forms of violence.[10] The term sexual misconduct is a problematic and political term. It reflects the history of treating sexual assault and harassment as simply one of many forms of misconduct. In fact, many national militaries—including Canada's and Australia's—did not collect regular and disaggregated data on sexual misconduct until 2008 in Australia and 2015 in Canada. Instead, incidents of sexual misconduct were simply included in general data on all forms of misconduct. The term sexual misconduct is also distinct from civilian legal terms, such as sexual assault, sexual harassment, and sexual violence, which centres victims and frames the incident in terms of the experience of the act for victims rather than merely as a violation of a military code of conduct.

The CAF have failed to collect and publicize consistent and reliable data related to MSV. Methods of data for the CAF—similar to many other western militaries—are staggeringly inadequate, inconsistent, and haphazard and defy basic principles of data collection. Paying attention to the data on MSV is important because it helps signal the efforts the CAF put into understanding and addressing the problem. I argue that the history of data collection related to MSV signals a lack of commitment and possibly even a concerted effort to obscure the extent of the problem. It is impossible to know the intent behind data collection practices; however, it is possible to conclude that, up until the past few years the CAF did not have enough information to even understand the scope of the problem of MSV, let alone address it. I argue that data collection is political and the lack of effort to collect and make public clear data should be taken as a signal of a lack of commitment to addressing the problem. In the next paragraph, I outline what data is available in the Canadian context. I preface this discussion by noting that, in addition to the limits on available sources of data, there is also evidence of a culture of underreporting, particularly among women. Research from other contexts suggests that only 15% of victims of MSV report the incident[11]; therefore, all incident and survey data discussed below should be read with the understanding that these are likely the tip of the iceberg in terms of total number of victims.

The 2016 Survey on Sexual Misconduct in the Canadian Armed Forces (SSMCAF) found 27% of women in the armed forces had been sexually assaulted in their careers, and members of the CAF were twice as likely to be sexually assaulted compared to the general population. It was also found that female regular force members are four times more likely than males to report and are more likely to identify their supervisor or other higher-ranking personnel as the perpetrator. Another survey was released in 2018, with similar findings; a notable difference was that 30% of regular force members reported fearing negative consequences of reporting MSV. The 2016 survey was initiated after former Supreme Court Justice Marie Deschamps conducted an external review of this issue and is scheduled to be conducted every 2 years. Prior to the 2016 survey, one of the only sources of data on MSV came from a Statistics Canada survey on Canadian community health. This survey was not intended to measure MSV in the forces but does include references and some statistics as part of the larger survey of mental health in the CAF. Unfortunately, this information is not currently publicly available. There is not much data on MSV at military colleges, with the exception of a 2019 Statistics Canada survey and report.

In Canada, the media have been an important source of MSV data and media reporting has highlighted the gaps in data on this issue. News articles going back to the 1990s contain a variety of personal stories, estimates of numbers of sexual assaults, and data from freedom of information requests. The series of investigative articles published by Maclean's Magazine (starting in 1998) provide important insight into the prevalence of MSV prior to any formal collection of data. The remainder of the chapter will highlight how zero tolerance statements are a key feature in media coverage of MSV. The next section defines zero tolerance statements; this is followed by an overview of high-profile cases of MSV in Canada and examples of the zero tolerance statements from senior leaders that followed these events.

Zero Tolerance Statements

Zero tolerance statements are statements made by military leaders or government officials indicating that the institution has 'zero tolerance' for MSV or has a policy of 'zero tolerance' for such conduct. I define MSV zero tolerance statements as a rhetorical tool because they are used strategically—often after media attention to high-profile cases of MSV to establish or revive trust and assurance that the institution is effectively handling the problem of MSV. In my 2023 book, *Good Soldiers Don't Rape: The Stories We Tell About Military Sexual Violence*, I use 30 years of media analysis to map out how and when zero tolerance statements are used.[12] I searched media coverage in top Canadian print outlets between 1989 and 2017 for the instances when officials were quoted using the following phrases of 'zero tolerance,' 'no tolerance,' and 'not tolerated.' The results do not indicate all instances of zero tolerance statements, but they do provide a strong sense of the pattern associated with these statements. The number of zero tolerance statements identified in the 30-year period in Canada was 44 and the graph below shows the distribution across all media coverage.

Zero tolerance statements were almost exclusively published in the aftermath of high-profile sexual misconduct cases, or cases that received significant media attention. Following high-profile cases of sexual misconduct there was often a surge in news articles taking a "change" frame and using a range of rhetorical phrases to signal institutional commitment to addressing this MSV. In articles where military or government officials were quoted, there was often an emphasis on the introduction of 'new rules,' a 'new focus,' a 'new wave,' or 'zero tolerance.' The overarching message of articles relying on these phrases was that military sexual violence was something the military was 'tackling' effectively and had control over.

I classify the publication or reference to zero tolerance statements as a rhetorical tool because they are published with no supporting evidence to attest to the zero tolerance commitment. The message often is that the institution has a commitment to zero tolerance, which may reassure readers or alleviate the sense of concern that any individual case or data related to MSV might raise. Zero tolerance statements did not only come in the form of direct quotes by military and government officials. Rather, journalists used the phrase to reiterate existing commitments or echo claims made by officials.

There are several features of most articulations of zero tolerance. First, zero tolerance statements claim that change is imminent. Zero tolerance references tend to emphasize the presumed progressive, aggressive, and effective responses of the military to sexual assault, and the implied positive changes the institution is making in this regard. The message conveyed to the public is that action and change is occurring. A second feature of zero tolerance statements is the confident, aggressive, strident, and even bombastic tone. Zero tolerance statements seem designed to signal to the public: "don't worry, we have this under control." Zero tolerance is equated with a 'tough on sexual misconduct' approach that draws on military metaphors to signal that the institution is 'tackling' the issue, is winning the battle with this issue, and has a clear plan of attack for dealing with this issue. This echoes other forms of policy rhetoric such as the 'war on drugs,' which position aggressive responses against previous 'weak' failures. The military institution is positioned as competent, strategic, and emphatically against misconduct, while the problem of misconduct is described as individual or isolated weakness or failings. A third feature of zero tolerance statements is that they often refer to a zero tolerance 'policy' or 'strategy,' yet rarely clarify what zero tolerance means in terms of specific institutional policies and practices. In addition, they often do not signal which set of policies or initiatives constitute a 'zero tolerance policy' or commitment. There is no actual 'zero tolerance' policy in Canada, yet officials regularly reference such a policy. In the following section, I outline defining and high-profile cases and events related to MSV in Canada. Examples of zero tolerance statements are included to signal the consistent pattern of these statements.

Defining Cases and Policy Evolution Related to MSV

Most western militaries—including the CAF—have had a number of high-profile cases of MSV that have largely shaped the national debate on the issue. In this section, I present the high-profile cases and major policy changes that have shaped Canadian discussions of MSV and have received the most significant amount of attention. I begin with a graph that captures media coverage between 1989 and 2017. I match the 'peaks' in media coverage with explanations of each incident associated with the coverage. This is followed by a brief discussion of the most recent series of high-profile cases of MSV that have occurred within the CAF, and examples of the zero tolerance statements that followed these events[13] (Fig. 1).

Figure 2 shows a clear pattern of increased media attention and then a cascade of zero tolerance statements in the weeks and months following the incident or incidents. This pattern to the timing of zero tolerance statements indicated to me that they were used strategically to respond and send a message to the public following a high-profile case. A deeper analysis of the content of these statements supports the argument that zero tolerance statements were used as a rhetorical tool to alleviate public concern about MSV following a high-profile case and send messages that MSV is not a problem, or is a problem already being addressed by the institution.

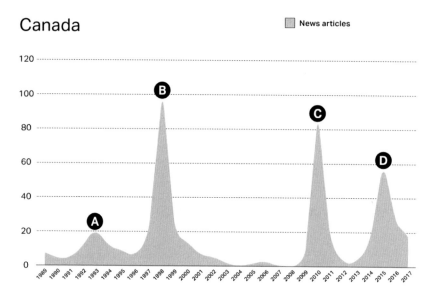

Fig. 1 Canada defining scandals

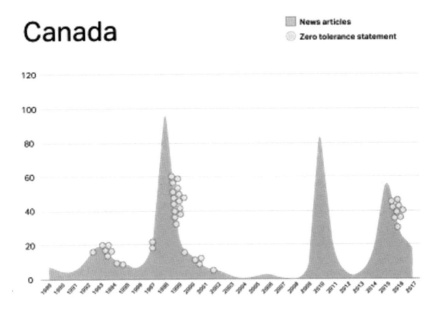

Fig. 2 Zero tolerance statements found in media coverage of MSV in Canada

Defining Cases and Zero Tolerance Statements

Department of National Defence Internal Survey and Human Rights Complaints

The small increase in media attention to MSV in Canada in 1993 (A) was the result of data published from a 1992 Department of National Defence internal survey, which reported that a quarter of service women experienced sexual harassment at work. It is important to remember that this period was when the CAF was also facing the Somalia inquiry so some articles linked the issues of sexual harassment to broader issues of discrimination—particularly racism and evidence of white supremacy within the CAF.[14] In 1993, media attention also centred on the annual report of the Canadian Human Rights Commission, which found that 13 of the 128 complaints related to sexual harassment brought to the commission were from the military—the highest number of any federal institution.

In 1993 then Captain Marc Rouleau, a spokesman for the defence department was quoted as saying the department had taken action to resolve problems related to MSV: "Action is being taken on the incidents that were outlined to make sure that they do not happen again. We have a zero-tolerance policy on harassment."[15] Around the same time, when then Prime Minister Brian Mulroney was accused of not addressing MSV, he stated: "The policy of all governments, including this one, has to be zero tolerance for sexual harassment."[16]

1998: Maclean's Magazine Feature Article

In 1998, Maclean's magazine published an exposé on MSV in the Canadian Forces that featured the stories of several survivors; it garnered significant national and international attention. Maclean's then published three follow up cover stories highlighting the systemic nature of MSV in the CAF. It is important to note that this came several years after the infamous 'Tailhook' case in the US, which was largely seen to have uncovered the significance of the problem of MSV in the US and initiated a trend in centring the voices of victims of MSV. The Maclean's articles are seen as directly contributing to a proposed policy change to have sexual assault cases become the jurisdiction of the military justice system.

Following the Maclean's feature, then defence minister Art Eggleton told the House of Commons that the military has a "zero tolerance" policy regarding abuse, going on to say: "Those people who are perpetrators of sexual abuse, we do not want them to be a part of the Canadian Forces."[17] In 1998, then Prime Minister Jean Chrétien also signalled his government's commitment to a 'zero-tolerance policy' towards harassment in the Canadian Forces. This same year, when speaking about sexual misconduct, retired LCol Shirley Robinson called out military leaders for using 'zero tolerance' rhetoric: "They keep talking about zero tolerance and all this good stuff. But I haven't heard anything about any of these guys being turfed out of the armed forces".[18] .

2010: Colonel Russell Williams Scandal

In 2010, Russel Williams, a previous commander at CFB Trenton, was charged with murdering two 38-year-old women, two home invasions that included forced confinement and sexual assaults, and 82 incidents of break and enter. The story drew intense media coverage because of the brutal nature of the murders, the number of victims, and the details of the perpetrator's underwear fetish. This case also highlighted issues of power abuse between commanders and lower-ranking service members and showed limitations to a system of reporting and justice that would allow for a perpetrator to commit so many crimes before being arrested.

2013–2017

There were a series of events between 2013 and 2017 that garnered increased media attention to MSV. The first was the publication of results from the 2013 Canadian Forces Mental Health Survey that sought to measure rates of post-traumatic stress disorder (PTSD) and sexual assault experiences.[19] At the time, the CAF used the term "military work-related sexual assault" (MWSA) and found that 14.8% of service members experienced unwanted touching, 7.6% experienced forced sexual activity, and 15.5% experienced sexual assault in a workplace-related setting. Over 90% of all of these recorded instances were committed by another CAF member or DND employee.

In 2014, *Maclean's* and *L'Actualité* co-published another high-profile exposé entitled 'Our military's disgrace.' This exposé focused on Stephanie Raymond, who had accused former Warrant Officer André Gagnon of assaulting her. Raymond was dismissed soon after she filed the complaint with military police in 2012. After repeated appeals, Gagnon was charged and the Chief of the Defence Staff issued an apology and admitted the CAF had failed in their handling of the case. In addition to featuring Raymond's case, *Maclean's/L'Actualité* featured the stories of dozens of victims of MSV and the results of extensive research into data and processes related to MSV in the CAF. Partly in response to the attention generated by the features, the CAF called for an external review led by former Supreme Court Justice Marie Deschamps.[20]

In 2015, former Justice Marie Deschamps was tasked with conducting an external review of policies, procedures, and programmes in relation to sexual harassment and assault. After interviews and focus groups that included over 700 participants, Justice Deschamps issued her external review, which became widely referred to as 'the Deschamps Report.' The report found an 'underlying sexualized culture in the CAF that is hostile to women and LGBTQ members.' It also found that as members moved up the ranks, they became desensitized to this culture. The report also found that the current policies and claims of 'zero tolerance' were insufficient, and that the CAF had not adequately defined, collected data on, or understood the nature of the problem of MSV. The Deschamps report included 10 key recommendations, the foremost of which was to establish an independent body that would handle MSV complaints, data collection, justice, and victim support .

Following the publication of the Deschamps report, the CAF issued 'Operation HONOUR,' which was a series of policies and strategies designed to change the culture in the Forces and stop inappropriate sexual behaviours. It was launched by then Chief of the Defence Staff Jonathan Vance, who later faced multiple allegations of MSV. Operation HONOUR used militarized language and metaphors to describe a "mission" to eliminate sexual misconduct. After the 2015 launch, there was an increase in reports of sexually inappropriate behaviour (40 reports in 2015, 300 reports in 2017). An internal report (2018) described this increase as evidence that service members trusted the system; however, internal data also indicated service members did not trust the system and 30% feared negative reprisal for reporting MSV.

As part of Operation HONOUR, the Statistics Canada Survey on Sexual Misconduct in the Canadian Armed Forces was initiated in 2016.[21] As indicated earlier, the survey found 27% of women in the armed forces had been sexually assaulted in their careers, and members of the CAF were twice as likely to be sexually assaulted compared to the general population. It also found that female regular force members were four times more likely than males to report and were more likely to identify their supervisor or other higher-ranking personnel as the perpetrator. Another survey was released in 2018, with similar findings; a notable difference was that 30% of regular force members reported fearing negative consequences of reporting MSV. In response to the Deschamps report, in 2016 the Canadian Forces Strategic Response Team and the Sexual Misconduct Response Centre were established.

In 2017, the *Globe & Mail* released findings of 20 months' worth of investigations into MSV in the CAF. The report included one of the clearest insights into the scope of the problem; it presented data from 870 police forces, provided detailed insights into the military justice process, and highlighted key inadequacies of the system identified by victims of MSV. As a result of the report, 179 cases of sexual misconduct were reviewed, and 23 cases were re-opened.

During this period, media coverage highlighted the rhetoric of zero tolerance that had been used in the past and noted the lack of progress. An editorial in the Toronto Star in 2015 concluded: "for decades the military brass claimed to champion "zero tolerance" for such abuses, despite all evidence to the contrary. If Gen. Vance accomplishes nothing else in his stint at the top, he will do the ranks a service by coming down hard on this poisonous threat to morale and cohesiveness."[22] Then Chief of the Defence Staff (CDS) Jonathan Vance consistently stated that the CAF had a zero tolerance approach: "For me it's simple. What's important is that victims and survivors get the support and help they need, and that we act decisively to deal with perpetrators."[23]

From 2019 to Present

2019: MSV Class Action Lawsuit
Following the Deschamps report in 2015 there was a wave of class action lawsuits filed across Canada on behalf of those who had experienced assault, harassment, or gender-based discrimination in the CAF. In 2017, the Canadian government declared that it did not owe a "private law duty of care to members within the CAF to provide a safe and harassment-free work environment or to create policies to prevent sexual harassment or sexual assault." This caused a social backlash and government lawyers agreed to settle out of court. In 2019, the Federal Court of Canada agreed to settle a $900 million class action lawsuit for victims of sexual assault employed by the Canadian military or the Department of National Defence. The settlement will provide payments of between $5000 and $55,000 for victims. The period for victims to come forward with claims was between 25 May 2020 and 24 November 2021; as of April 2021, over 4,600 individuals had filed claims dating as far back as the 1980s. The settlement not only provides compensation, but an opportunity for individuals to detail their experiences. It is important to note that the lawsuit claims that MSV is a systemic issue but the government does not admit liability through the lawsuit, nor has it offered any formal apology. As part of the settlement, policy changes and new programmes will be put into place, including a "restorative engagement" process where members can share their experiences of sexual misconduct with senior military leadership.

2019: R. v. Beaudry Settled
In 2019, the Supreme Court of Canada (SCC) heard a case that centred on whether service members had the constitutional right to a civilian jury trial for serious charges like sexual assault. The case related to Master Corporal Raphael Beaudry, who was convicted of sexual assault and

choking a victim. He appealed his conviction by standing court martial and requested a jury trial. In the appeal process, the Court Martial Appeal Court of Canada (CMAC) deemed that Beaudry's court martial was unconstitutional because he was being tried for an offence under the *Criminal Code*, not under military law. This was taken to the SCC, which ruled 5-2 to uphold the established system of military justice, which prevents service members from accessing civilian jury trials. This decision was significant and highlighted several debates related to MSV, including whether a separate justice system for the military is appropriate and effective, and whether service members and victims should have a right to trial by jury, as guaranteed to Canadians under the Charter of Rights and Freedoms.

2021: Two Chief of the Defence Staffs and Other Senior Leaders Accused of MSV

In July 2020, then CDS Vance announced his retirement after a 5-year term in the role, which included launching Operation HONOUR in 2015.[24] He was replaced by Vice-Admiral Art McDonald. Several months later, in February 2021, Kellie Brennan, a former service member who retired as a major, came forward with allegations that she had an ongoing relationship with Vance for decades. She reported the relationship to the military police and was featured in a video interview on Global News. She claimed the relationship started in 2001 and continued when Vance was CDS. She described Vance as having abused his power and claimed that although it was initially consensual, given the power imbalance in their rank, she felt unable to 'say no' to him.

In a parliamentary committee meeting that examined the matter, former military ombudsman Gary Walbourne announced that he had warned defence minister Harjit Sajjan about a separate MSV allegation involving Vance in 2018. Walbourne claimed that the minister refused to take an envelope with evidence related to the allegation. Further parliamentary committee meetings and reports found that Minister Sajjan referred the matter to the Privy Council Office and also discussed the possible allegations with staff in the Prime Minister's Office; however, Prime Minister Trudeau claims that he was not made aware of the allegations by his Chief of Staff and learned of them through media reports in 2021. As a result of the onslaught of allegations against senior leaders, OPERATION Honour was suspended in March 2021 and is expected to be replaced with a new series of policies.[25]

During the investigation of Vance's case, he was accused of obstruction of justice for reaching out to the victim and encouraging her to lie about the case. Vance pleaded guilty to obstruction of justice. The judge concluded: "I don't feel it's necessary to burden you with a criminal conviction" and Vance was given a conditional discharge with 80 hours of community service and no criminal record.[26]

In late February 2021—after less than two months in the job—the officer who replaced Jonathan Vance, Admiral McDonald, stepped aside after allegations of sexual misconduct against him were raised. The allegations dated back to 2010. McDonald denied the allegations and the investigation ended without a charge. The Trudeau government dismissed McDonald shortly thereafter. Following McDonald's dismissal, there were a number of charges raised against senior CAF leaders, including Vice-Admiral Hayden Edmundson, the former head of military personnel. Edmundson took leave without pay from March 2021 as he faced an investigation over an historic allegation of rape. As of April 2023, the case was awaiting trial. Another senior leader, Maj. Gen. Dany Fortin, the head of Canada's vaccine logistics at the Public Health Agency Canada, was removed from his position in 2021 under allegations related to a historic case of sexual misconduct. Fortin was found not guilty of the allegations in 2022 and lodged a $6 million lawsuit against members of the Canadian government and CAF leaders in 2023.

In April 2021, former Supreme Court Justice Louise Arbour was appointed to conduct an external review of sexual harassment and misconduct in the military. Part of her mandate was to focus on how the military can create an independent reporting system for sexual misconduct. In 2022, Justice Arbour released her report, which included 48 recommendations designed to help the CAF address its systemic sexual violence problem. Defence minister Anita Anand responded with a commitment to treat the report as a 'roadmap' and implement all recommendations over time.

Conclusion

To conclude, this chapter has demonstrated how government and military leaders respond in predictable ways to the type of high-profile cases listed above. Specifically, leaders consistently make claims of 'zero tolerance' to MSV following such cases. These statements are used as a way to mitigate public concern, establish authority, and convey a sense that the institution is handling the crisis. It is possible to observe a clear pattern of crisis, zero tolerance statement, public appeasement, and inaction over the past few decades in Canada. Such an analysis puts the current MSV crisis in Canada in context and serves as a warning that so-called watershed moments do not always lead to significant and impactful change. Instead, high-profile cases are often merely followed by rhetoric of zero tolerance and vague commitments to change. The following section explains what is meant by 'zero tolerance statements' in further detail.

This pattern of high-profile case followed by commitments to zero tolerance helps put the current MSV crisis in historic context and dampens any expectations that this might truly be a watershed moment that will necessarily evoke radical change in the CAF. One difference with the current crisis is that the current Minister of National Defence, Anita Anand, has made the strongest and most consistent commitments to addressing MSV of any minister or military leader. The fact that she agreed, in principle, to commit to all of Justice Arbour's 48 recommendations is cause for optimism. However, this optimism should be tempered with the reality that no Canadian Prime Minister has effectively championed this issue or continued their commitment to change beyond the initial crisis moment of high-profile cases.

Following the 2020/2021 series of high-profile cases of MSV, when asked to comment on yet another Canadian Armed Forces sexual misconduct scandal, Prime Minister Justin Trudeau said the military "simply doesn't get it."[27] Trudeau seemed to be trying to separate himself from the CAF's dysfunction and preserve his reputation as a feminist leader who does "get it." This is slightly different from previous 'zero tolerance' statements in that Trudeau seemed to be placing the blame on the armed forces, while absolving himself and his government of responsibility for solving the crisis.

Canada is not a military dictatorship, which means that responsibility for ensuring the military institution is functional sits squarely on the shoulders of the Prime Minister and Minister of National Defence. But in 2020 and 2021, they largely deferred and delayed handling the problem through calls for more investigations and reviews and claim the military are the 'the proper authorities' when it comes to addressing this issue.

The recent series of MSV crises in the CAF must be put within a historic context. There are currently so many senior leaders on leave, under investigation, or facing allegations of sexual misconduct that it is dizzying. What is absolutely clear is that sexual misconduct is a systemic problem and that the CAF's top leaders are not only incapable of handling the problem, they are deeply implicated in it. All too often, those looking for a silver lining to sexual misconduct ask if this is just a generational, old boy's problem. The hope is that once young and more progressive leaders get into positions of power, there will be less misogyny and systemic sexual violence.

But sexual misconduct is not a generational issue—it is a deeply engrained cultural problem that reproduces itself. At the heart of this problem are beliefs and practices that position women and femininity as weak, while heralding a type of masculinity that celebrates the use of violence and the display of power through aggression. When this is combined with military exceptionalism—or the widespread belief that military service is unique and service members should be held to separate standards to civilians—a military culture that is defined by both sexism and impunity is fostered. Within this culture, older generations of old boys are replaced with new old boys that share the same objective: to sustain a sexist system of impunity, and their power within it, at all costs.

While previous generations of service members and political leaders thrived in a work environment where overt sexual misconduct and harassment was openly written off as "jokes," hazing, or a valued part of "building character" and camaraderie, the new generation of military and political old boys has more sophisticated techniques. These include declarations of zero tolerance of misconduct in the face of ample evidence of institutional tolerance, statements supporting cultural change with no resources or actual plans to support this change, quietly moving abusive service members to other roles, and gaslighting victims and encouraging them not to come forward lest they ruin their careers.

It is time to stop looking to the dysfunctional CAF for solutions to the sexual misconduct crisis and trace both the source of the problem and the person responsible for fixing it back to the Prime Minister. True political leadership that lasts beyond crisis moments has the potential to reduce MSV and break the cycle of scandal, zero tolerance statement, and inaction that has plagued the CAF for decades.

Notes

1. Australian Human Rights Commission (2013).
2. Philipps (2021).
3. Connolly (2021).

4. Gallant (2021).
5. Mulrine (2012) and DART (2016, p. 31).
6. Wilson (2020).
7. Francis (2013).
8. Rico (2017).
9. Government of Canada (2022).
10. Government of Canada (2021).
11. DART (2016, p. 31) and Australian Human Rights Commission (2012).
12. MacKenzie (2023).
13. For a more complete history of military culture and MSV in the CAF, please see Charlotte Duval-Lantoine, *The Ones We Let Down: Toxic Leadership Culture and Gender Integration in the Canadian Forces* (Montreal: McGill University Press) 2022.
14. In 1993, news broke of Canadian soldiers torturing and killing Somali children and teenagers while on a humanitarian mission in Somalia. The acts were documented by photographs and further details of the incidents came out following a public inquiry. The torture and abuse became popularly referred to as the 'Somalia affair' and 'Somalia inquiry,' with the inquiry revealing broader forms of systemic abuse and sexism in the CAF.
15. York (1993).
16. Toronto Star (1993).
17. Toronto Star (1998).
18. Murray (1998).
19. Zamorski et al. (2016).
20. Blatchford (2015).
21. Government of Canada (2016)
22. Toronto Star (2015).
23. MacCharles (2016).
24. Brewster (2020).
25. Brewster (2021).
26. Connolly (2022).
27. Raycraft (2021).

REFERENCES

Australian Human Rights Commission. 2012. *Review into the Treatment of Women in the Australian Defence Force*. Phase 2 Report.

Australian Human Rights Commission. 2013. Australian Human Rights Commission.

Blatchford, Christie. 2015. Troubling Report Blasts Military; Inflammatory: Former Judge Finds Mirror Stories in Maclean's and L'actualite, Without Names. *Vancouver Sun*.

Brewster, Murray. 2020. Gen. Jonathan Vance, Chief of the Defence Staff, Announces Retirement. CBC News. Available at: https://www.cbc.ca/news/politics/vance-retiring-chief-of-the-defence-staff-1.5660106.

Brewster, Murray. 2021. Campaign to End Sexual Harassment in Canadian Armed Forces Shut Down. CBC News. Available at: https://www.cbc.ca/news/politics/operation-honour-closed-down-1.5962978.

Connolly, Amanda. 2021. Military Sexual Misconduct Class Action Claims Soar to 13,500 as Deadline Nears. Global News.

Connolly, Amanda. 2022. Gen. Jonathan Vance Pleads Guilty to Obstruction of Justice, Gets Conditional Discharge. Global News. Available at: https://globalnews.ca/news/8720429/jonathan-vance-guilty-plea-obstruction-of-justice/.

DART. 2016. Final Report. Barton: Defence Abuse Response Taskforce.

Duval-Lantoine, Charlotte. 2022. *The Ones We Let Down: Toxic Leadership Culture and Gender Integration in the Canadian Forces*. Montreal: McGill University Press.

Francis, David. 2013. Military Sexual Assaults Cost More Than $872 Million. *The Fiscal Times*.

Gallant, Jacques. 2021. Almost 19,000 Claims Submitted in Canadian Military Sexual Misconduct Lawsuits. *Toronto Star*.

Government of Canada. 2016. Sexual Misconduct in the Canadian Armed Forces, 2016. Available at: https://www150.statcan.gc.ca/n1/pub/85-603-x/85-603-x2016001-eng.htm.

Government of Canada. 2021. DAOD 9005–1, Sexual Misconduct Response.

Government of Canada, Department of National Defence. 2022. Training and Educational Materials About Sexual Misconduct.

MacCharles, Tonda. 2016. Canadian Armed Forces Punish 30 for Sexual Misconduct in Military Ranks. *Toronto Star*. Available at: https://www.thestar.com/news/canada/2016/08/30/canadian-forces-punish-30-for-sexual-misconduct-in-military-ranks.html.

MacKenzie, Megan. 2023. *Good Soldiers Don't Rape: The Stories We Tell About Military Sexual Violence*. London: Cambridge University Press.

Mulrine, Anna. 2012. Pentagon Report: Sexual Assault in the Military Up Dramatically. *The Christian Science Monitor*. Available at: www.csmonitor.com/USA/Military/2012/0119/Pentagon-report-Sexualassault-in-the-military-up-dramatically.

Murray, M. 1998. New Training Bids to Cut Harassment Officer Points to Special Lessons All Ranks Must Take. *The Toronto Star*.

Philipps, Dave. 2021. Military Missteps Allowed Soldier Accused of Murder to Flee, Report Says. *New York Times*. Available at: www.nytimes.com/2021/04/30/us/vanessa-guillen-fort-hood-aaron-robinson.html.

Raycraft, Richard. 2021 Military 'Simply Doesn't Get It' When It Comes to Sexual Misconduct, PM Says. CBC News. Available at: https://www.cbc.ca/news/politics/military-doesnt-get-it-sexual-misconduct-1.6201648.

Rico, Antonieta. 2017. Why Military Women Are Missing from the #MeToo Movement. *Time Magazine*.

Toronto Star. 1993. Race Hatred Alive in Canada, Rights Head Says.

Toronto Star. 1998. More Sex Abuse Reports Emerge in Wake of Article Defence Minister Calls Behaviour "Unacceptable".

Toronto Star. 2015. Gen. Vance's Search-and-Destroy Mission Targets Sexual Misconduct: Editorial. Available at: https://www.thestar.com/opinion/editorials/2015/08/18/gen-vances-search-and-destroy-mission-targets-sexual-misconduct-editorial.html.

Wilson, Cam. 2020. Australia's Defence Forces Have Spent $50 Million On Sexual Abuse Claims in the Past Three Years. Pedestrian Group.

York, G. 1993. Sex Harassment Called Rampant on Military Bases Federal Report Says Complaining Carries Risk of Serious Harm. *The Globe and Mail*.

Zamorski, Mark A., Rachel Bennett, David Boulos, Bryan Garber, Rakesh Jetly, and Jitender Sareen. 2016. The 2013 Canadian Forces Mental Health Survey. *Canadian Journal of Psychiatry* 61 (1): 10S–25S.

Canadian Armed Forces Reconstitution: The Critical Role of Personnel Retention

Irina Goldenberg and Nancy Otis

People are at the core of everything the Canadian Armed Forces (CAF) does to deliver on its mandate. The extensive training, education, and socialization that CAF members receive to imbue them with specialized military knowledge and skills needed to meet the unique demands of military service make personnel the CAF's most important asset, and personnel retention one of the CAF's top strategic priorities.[1] Therefore, it is imperative that the CAF protects its considerable investment in the expertise and knowledge of its people.

Unlike most organizations, militaries invest significant resources in employee training and have unique job requirements that can only be met through experience obtained in the organization. Lateral entry is generally not possible, which makes the direct costs of turnover high. Indirect costs, such as lower morale, lost productivity, lost corporate

I. Goldenberg (✉) · N. Otis
Ottawa, ON, Canada
e-mail: Irina.goldenberg@forces.gc.ca

N. Otis
e-mail: Nancy.Otis@forces.gc.ca

© The Author(s), under exclusive license to Springer Nature Switzerland AG 2023
T. Juneau and P. Lagassé (eds.), *Canadian Defence Policy in Theory and Practice, Volume 2*, Canada and International Affairs, https://doi.org/10.1007/978-3-031-37542-2_3

memory, and the added workload on those remaining, compound retention concerns. Meanwhile, preventing attrition of trained personnel is getting harder in today's competitive job market.[2] Like other militaries, the CAF has suffered from reduced intake and training capacity as a result of the pandemic and an organizational culture crisis.[3] The CAF's commitments to operations and international peace and security have further contributed to burnout and exhaustion, challenging CAF readiness and the military personnel system.[4]

As a result, the CAF has undertaken the CAF Reconstitution initiative to return to 71,500 Regular Force and 30,000 Reserve Force members, as originally outlined in the 2017 defence policy *Strong, Secure, Engaged*, or *SSE*.[5] Reconstitution comprises a number of simultaneous strategic objectives, including modernizing recruitment, streamlining training and other personnel production requirements, and increasing diversity,[6] with a fundamental focus on personnel retention. A key strategic initiative of Reconstitution is the CAF Retention Strategy, which aims "to improve retention and reduce unhealthy attrition."[7]

This chapter provides an overview of recent research on the multitude of personal, organizational, and societal variables that influence CAF attrition and retention, which is often understood as the outcome of a number of factors such as job satisfaction, well-being, organizational commitment, and identity.[8] Equally important, militaries have an intricate personnel management system, comprising a multitude of subgroups of personnel that can be analysed from a range of perspectives (e.g., component, environment or service, military occupation, geographic location, rank, and family status). To offer some insights into how organizations can tackle this complex challenge, we present key enablers of retention as well as some examples of retention initiatives and strategies that were recently implemented in the CAF.

Does the CAF Has a Retention Problem?

Looking at overall release rates, CAF attrition is not particularly high, remaining between 8 and 9% annually, with 3% expected each year from retirements alone.[9] The CAF's overall attrition rate is also lower than that of allied armed forces, including the United Kingdom (9.4%), Australia (9%), and New Zealand (8.5%).[10] Moreover, CAF attrition is generally comparable to or lower than the Canadian labour market rate reported by the Conference Board of Canada, including in both the private (10.2%) and public sectors (4.7%).[11]

However, looking more closely reveals higher, and in some cases very concerning, rates of attrition within specific CAF subgroups, which affects readiness and causes challenges for the organization. While we will delve deeper into specific aspects later in the chapter, these subgroups include:

- Differences in attrition by years of service: Concerning rates of attrition among new members during their first year of service and in the most tenured members with greater than 20 years of service.[12]
- Gender differences: Overall rates of attrition are lower for women than for men, but there are consistent differences in the type of attrition, with women being more likely to release due to medical reasons.[13]
- Occupational differences: Some CAF occupations (e.g., technical or health services) have much higher attrition rates than others, affecting the overall readiness of the force.[14]
- Location differences: Remote and rural locations have higher attrition,[15] creating personnel shortages at specific bases and wings.
- Component differences: Attrition rates are higher in the Reserve Force than in the Regular Force.[16]

Types of Turnover and Retention

It is important to distinguish different types of personnel turnover. The most basic distinction is that between *voluntary turnover*, which occurs when employees freely choose to leave their jobs, and *involuntary turnover*, which occurs when employees are terminated for reasons such as disciplinary concerns, cutbacks, or mandatory retirement. Another important distinction is that between *avoidable turnover*, stemming from factors such as job dissatisfaction or more enticing employment elsewhere, and *unavoidable turnover*, due to health issues, for example. Not all turnover is undesirable, and indeed some attrition can be beneficial: *functional turnover* happens when a poor performer decides to leave, whereas *dysfunctional turnover* refers to cases in which high-performing employees leave. Nonetheless, even functional turnover carries costs in recruiting, hiring, and training new employees. In sum, problematic turnover can be understood as that which is voluntary, avoidable, and dysfunctional; this subset of turnover is negative and yet actionable, which is where organizations can focus their retention efforts.

Organizational Commitment

Organizational commitment has been demonstrated to have a critical influence on retention and is probably the most researched attitudinal construct in this domain.[17] The main model of commitment is Meyer and Allan's three-dimensional model,[18] according to which *affective commitment* refers to one's emotional bond to the organization, *normative commitment* refers to feelings of obligation or duty to remain in the organization, and *continuance commitment* reflects attachment to the organization due to a lack of other alternatives or because of losses associated with leaving (e.g., seniority, pension, or close ties to co-workers).

A wealth of research shows that employees high in affective and normative commitment are more likely to remain in the organization, whereas continuous commitment appears to be unrelated or to have a slight negative relation to retention, especially when affective and continuous commitment are low. All three types of commitment relate to functional retention: affectively and normatively committed personnel are more likely to stay, are more motivated to perform, and tend to contribute positively. In contrast, continuously committed personnel with low affective and normative commitment are stuck in a job with few alternatives and may be unmotivated, cynical, and low contributors. Of course, one can be high or low on any or all of these forms of commitment because they can function independently. Thus, it is optimal for CAF members to evince high levels of all three types of commitment: strong emotional ties to the force, a strong sense of duty to serve, and to feel that they have good pay, benefits, and various non-monetary conditions and experiences that they would not get outside of the military.[19]

Multifaceted Nature of Retention

Understanding retention is not a simple matter, and a variety of factors have been identified at the individual, occupational, and organizational levels, as illustrated in Fig. 1.

Teasing out the causal factors underpinning retention is challenging. Retention and attrition occur in a complex, multifactorial environment,

Fig. 1 Shortlist of factors related to retention

and people usually do not leave for one specific reason. The factors occurring at different levels include the following:

- Individual, psychological, and personality differences (i.e., people's various needs, wants, and preferences).
- Individual demographic factors such as age, gender, and ethnicity (e.g., a single 22-year-old man's reasons for leaving will probably differ from those of a married 45-year-old woman).
- Organizational demographic variables such as component (Regular or Reserve Force), service or military environment (i.e., land, air, sea), rank, and military occupation. Cooks, infantry soldiers, naval engineers, pilots, and lawyers, for example, have different career paths in the CAF and different employment opportunities in the civilian labour market, so the factors that affect their leave decisions will differ as well.

- Internal conditions, including organizational practices and policies. For example, when the CAF changed the Invariable Engagement terms of service from 20 to 25 years, there was a predictable change in attrition in that the high rates of attrition previously observed at 20 years of service moved to 25 years of service.[20]
- External conditions are also critical. One of the most important factors is the external labour market. All things being equal, low unemployment will mean higher CAF attrition, and high unemployment will mean lower CAF attrition. The aging workforce, increasing cultural diversity, and changes in technology also affect military retention and attrition.[21]

Still, some drivers are more consequential than others, and there has been a lot of research on all these influencers.

Interface Between Recruitment and Retention

Recruitment and retention are closely connected, and they are primary lines of effort in CAF Reconstitution (in addition to training and production).[22] More often than not, when attrition is high or personnel manning is low, militaries increase recruitment.[23] As alluded to above, however, new and untrained personnel cannot replace trained and experienced members, and they cannot address rank structure targets and leader succession.[24]

In addition, accelerated recruitment makes it difficult to maintain the quality of recruits. Standards are sometimes lowered when recruitment needs are high (such as lowering cut-off scores on selection tests), which leads to a rise in training and performance failures and spikes in early attrition, compounding the retention problem.[25] Accelerated recruitment also results in increased pressure on the personnel generation systems, which has a domino effect. Long wait times for stages of training can affect new recruits' morale, increasing their risk of leaving.[26] It becomes harder for the system to direct recruits into occupations they are best suited to. Early attrition can also result from unrealistic job previews, mismatches between personal expectations and military culture and requirements, as well as inadequate socialization.[27] Taken together, increased recruitment is a poor response to attrition due to the high investment required to train and develop military personnel in the first place.

Generational and Cohort Considerations

Successful recruitment and retention require an understanding of generational and cohort differences. Different generations or cohorts approach work in different ways.[28] While they are likely to seek many of the same employment factors as previous generations (e.g., steady employment, respect, good pay, promotion, and self-development opportunities), post-millennials expect their careers to advance quickly, expect certain organizational policies and workplace practices, and to work with the latest tools and technologies.[29]

A comprehensive analysis of retaining upcoming generations in the armed forces highlights four important aspects[30]:

- They will be looking for participatory leadership and collaborative approaches to work and will have a greater sense of independence to act first and seek permission later. Thus, they are likely to be less deferent to authority, which could challenge systems with hierarchical leadership structures, such as the CAF, and leaders will likely need to better balance expectations of compliance with independence and recognition of multiple perspectives.
- They live in more culturally diverse contexts and will likely have internalized pluralism of cultures, belief systems, and normative behaviours compared with previous cohorts. As such, they are more likely to expect the military to balance its conformist culture with more flexible cultural expectations and a greater acceptance of ambiguity and freedom to choose among alternatives.
- While they are prepared to work, they are more likely to challenge the clock-punching culture of set hours and only doing work-related activities on the job. Militaries might benefit from examining ways of offering personnel greater flexibility and control over how, when, and even where they work. This is particularly important following the effects of the COVID-19 pandemic on approaches to work, including greater use of flexible and hybrid work options.[31]
- They will be slower to decide on a specific occupation and will be more likely to want to sample different options. Facilitating internal and even external mobility will likely require moving more strongly toward a competency-based personnel system that allows for flexible employment paths (e.g., occupational transfers, switching between

full-time and part-time service, and even periods of leave and re-enrolment). This would represent a major shift from the current career-ladder approach, but may be important for retention.

All in all, winning the battle for talent among millennial and post-millennial cohorts will likely require significant changes in military personnel management.

Component Perspective: Retention in the Regular and Reserve Forces

The CAF comprises Regular and Reserve Force components, with the Reserve Force made up of part-time personnel who complement and support Regular Force operations. Reservists can be employed in three different classes of service, and they often transition between them[32]: Class A service is non-operational, part-time, and generally involves training and employment for a minimum of two weeks a year and frequent weekend activities. Class B service is also non-operational but involves full-time contracts and is, in many ways, similar to Regular Force service but without some key conditions of service. Class C service is operational, full-time, and includes deployment domestically and internationally but, again, unlike for regulars, this deployment is voluntary, other than in extreme circumstances.[33]

Regular Force members and reservists evince significantly different reasons for releasing from the CAF. The main reasons Regular Force members release are job dissatisfaction, occupational dissatisfaction, impact of service life on spouses and children, and geographic instability and posting dissatisfaction. The main reasons Primary Reserve members release are impact on civilian employment, lack of meaningful work, and a greater desire for military service, including component transfers to the Regular Force.[34] Given that the CAF intends to enhance the role and capability of the Reserve Force and assign to Reserve Force units and formations new roles that provide the CAF with full-time capability through part-time service,[35] understanding both the common and unique concerns of personnel in this component is vital.[36]

Occupational Considerations in the Context of Military Service

The occupational perspective provides another important window on retention[37] because the CAF's 101 different occupations have different drivers of retention and attrition.[38] Not surprisingly, it is harder to retain personnel in occupations that are better paid and in high demand in the civilian world (e.g., technical and engineering occupations). As noted in the *CAF Retention Strategy*:

> Capabilities and skills that are in high demand across Canadian society are equally in high demand within the CAF. Technicians, medical specialists, logisticians, and those knowledgeable in developing technologies and specific domains, such as cyber operations, represent elements that speak to the requirement for focused retention: These individuals are challenging to recruit, critical to operational effectiveness, and possess skills in high demand across Canadian society.[39]

In addition, members in professional occupations, such as medical doctors, can experience conflicts between their professional identity and their military identity. For example, they may not be able to practice the full range of their professional skills within their military roles.[40] Other occupations deploy more frequently or for longer periods, so deployments may affect them more than others; conversely, some may lack deployment opportunities, and this too can be a source of dissatisfaction. Some military occupations may be perceived as more prestigious, including operational and specialist trades.[41] Some may be more hazardous and tend to have higher rates of injury.[42] Therefore, policymakers need to be mindful of the occupation-specific drivers of attrition as they develop and implement retention strategies. Thus, the latest report on recruitment and retention from the Office of the Auditor General recommended that the CAF "develop, implement, monitor, and evaluate measures to optimize retention for each occupation."[43]

Individual Demographic Differences

CAF members vary on a range of individual demographic variables (e.g., gender, race, ethnicity), each having their own individual lived experiences. The low attrition rate of the CAF overall can mask the loss of members within underrepresented populations and, of course, attrition of underrepresented groups impedes the CAF's ability to reach representation levels of individuals within these groups and leads to lower representation of underrepresented groups at senior levels.[44]

For the purposes of this strategy, the term "underrepresented" refers to those underrepresented in occupations and in the CAF as a whole (women, Indigenous peoples, visible minorities, people with disabilities, and LGBTQ2+ individuals). The CAF has established representation goals for women, Indigenous people, and visible minorities (25.1%, 3.5%, and 11%, respectively) set for 2026.[45] However, present rates of representation fall short of these goals.

The CAF is committed to being inclusive of all its current and future members. Efforts are underway to change the CAF culture to better support and reflect the needs of all who wish to serve (see the chapter by MacKenzie in this volume). It is the organization's responsibility to assess factors important for retaining members from underrepresented groups when developing a retention strategy and approaches.[46]

While in-depth analysis of retaining specific groups is beyond the scope of this chapter, some general reasons members of underrepresented populations leave include discrimination, implicit bias, harassment, or lack of a sense of belonging or even alienation due to lower inclusivity in the workplace.[47] Targeted retention efforts that focus on the issues and concerns of underrepresented groups are essential to ameliorating these issues. At the same time, broad cultural change is needed in the CAF to address these problems, an important focus for DND and the CAF at present.[48] The CAF Retention Strategy will work with other strategies and initiatives related to supporting diversity and culture change more broadly,[49] while developing targeted retention efforts to ensure that the needs of underrepresented groups are addressed.[50]

MILITARY FAMILIES AND THEIR ROLE IN CAF RETENTION

Addressing retention also means understanding the concerns of military members' families, who must make sacrifices in adapting to military life. The military has often been called a "greedy institution" because of the size and scope of the demands it makes on its members and their families.[51] Some of the main demands of military employment surround members being posted to locations of varying desirability, including remote and northern locations, which require them to relocate and move their families on a frequent basis. They often experience long absences from their homes and families as a result of training and deployments, and they put their lives on the line. Dual service couples are particularly affected, especially given that they may be required to be posted to different locations involving lengthy family separation,[52] and may experience even more extended separation from one another when taking deployment into account.[53] Moreover, given that approximately two-thirds of CAF women are part of a dual-service family (as compared to less than 10% of CAF men), family needs may disproportionately affect retention of women and exacerbate gender integration challenges.[54] On the other hand, military service can also be extremely rewarding, and military members and their families can become more resilient, and experience great fulfilment knowing they are contributing to their country.[55]

Research shows that family reasons are consistently near the top of CAF members' reasons for voluntary attrition,[56] and the extent to which families support the member's military service is consistently related to the member's decisions to stay or leave.[57] Thus, militaries need to continuously work on balancing the demands of service with family considerations, including developing family programmes and services to mitigate the known stresses of military life.

MILITARY RETENTION STRATEGIES AND INITIATIVES

Like many other militaries, the CAF has tried to build a *retention culture*—in other words, "an environment that encourages members to stay, to contribute, and to feel satisfied with their careers and valued by the organization."[58] This is a *relational approach* to retention, which can be contrasted with a *transactional approach*. Transactional incentives such as pay, benefits, and other concrete rewards will always be important. But research shows that the biggest influencers of retention in the armed forces are the relational aspects of military and service life.[59] These include consideration and respect for members and their families, fairness, recognition, leader support, and camaraderie—all these factors speak to the kind of organization that members want to belong to, and they strengthen members' affective and normative commitments.

Transactional and relational approaches have been contrasted as "buying low attrition versus building high retention,"[60] because research shows that financial incentives can bring short-term success but that transactional measures are not particularly effective in the long run, especially if applied without also taking relational measures into account. As discussed above, functional retention that reflects productivity, performance, and organizational well-being is about much more than numbers and attrition rates, and it is based on fostering personnel engagement and commitment through positive workplace practices and conditions.

Nonetheless, individual differences will always exist and what motivates one person will not necessarily motivate another. Some are interested in competitive salaries, others in educational opportunities, deployments, travel, or benefits for their family. This brings us to what a number of nations call the "Defence Employment Offer" or DEO, or in Canada "the CAF Offer."[61] DEOs include both the tangible and the intangible factors, the transactional as well as the relational, and they affect the reasons people join the military and the reasons they stay. Given the myriad individual differences, militaries need to better understand what benefits and work conditions influence commitment and retention, and then employ these in DEOs to maximize the value to both the member and the organization.

Retention on Two Fronts: Omnibus and Targeted Retention Strategies

It is clear that optimal retention depends on a two-level approach. At the general level, a broad range of personnel research reveals many common concerns (e.g., job satisfaction, leadership, family factors).[62] Thus, a CAF-wide or omnibus retention strategy is needed—a holistic CAF Offer that best balances the demands of service with members' needs. At a more granular level, the CAF needs targeted retention strategies to address unhealthy attrition in specific areas (e.g., first year of service; at-risk occupations). These will result in the highest return on investment and address critical shortages.[63] The next sections look at the enablers in more detail.

As noted when reflecting on post-millennial cohorts and equity-seeking groups, militaries must recognize the increased importance of flexibility and member choice that support members' career aspirations and their family's needs. A number of nations are looking at flexibility in the transition between full- and part-time (or reserve) service; an initiative coined "adaptive career path" in the CAF.[64] The intent of the adaptive career path, as indicated in *SSE*, is to "create an agile service model that supports transition between full- and part-time service and provides the flexibility to cater to differing Reserve career paths."[65]

Flexibility in retraining and changing occupations is another area that can have a significant impact. Component and occupational transfers provide members seeking change with options, and accommodating these career paths allows the military to retain valuable military skills and experience.[66]

The CAF is also examining increased flexibility in the principle of universality of service (DAOD 5023-0), which stipulates that all CAF members must be fit and ready to perform general military duties, not just the duties of their military occupation, which includes the requirement to meet fitness testing standards as well as to be deployable.[67] Amendments regarding strict adherence to this policy are currently being deliberated in order to support both reconstitution[68] and culture change objectives.[69]

A number of militaries are also exploring flexible work arrangements or "friendly employment policies" that enable members to better balance their military service with their family and other aspirations. These include working from home and variable working hours, compressed work weeks, part-time leave without pay, and sabbaticals or career breaks.

Another obvious enabler is leadership, which has a role to play at all levels.[70] Senior leaders must prioritize retention and ensure that strategies are developed at the organizational or strategic level, and then executed and resourced down the chain of command. Career or occupational leaders, such as branch authorities, need to identify and initiate actions to repair and sustain the career fields under their purview, because some attrition influencers are occupation-specific, as we discussed above. Unit commanders and school commandants need to maintain a positive workplace and get to know areas of concern to personnel, monitor local attrition, and take steps to address it in a location and context-specific manner. An example of a recent initiative is the standardized unit retention interview to assist unit commanders with discussing retention options with members who submitted a formal request for voluntary release.[71] Taken together, leadership's commitment to addressing the needs of their personnel and their families is a critical enabler of military retention.

Communication and transparency are also important retention enablers. The CAF already offers many benefits and has a highly competitive employment offer. But some drivers of dissatisfaction easily lend themselves to grass-is-greener thinking, so more is necessary to communicate and reinforce the transactional and relational benefits of CAF service. Recognizing that members need to be reminded of the various benefits beyond the attraction and recruitment stages, the CAF is developing the CAF Offer Interactive Guide that presents all information on compensation and benefits online.[72]

Research shows that a lack of communication up and down the chain of command is often a source of dissatisfaction among CAF members, who often feel that they are not getting pertinent information and that they are, for example, expected to perform without fully understanding how they fit into the mission.[73] CAF members also need to feel that their concerns are being relayed up the chain of command. If they feel that their supervisors are not advocating on their behalf and sharing their concerns, they can become cynical and disengaged.[74]

Finally, the organization needs to clearly communicate policies and changes. Research shows that perceptions of organizational fairness are extremely important: The actual benefits people get or do not get are less important than their believing that the processes behind the decision was fair.[75] Dispelling misconceptions and improving buy-in make clear and transparent communication vital to retention.

Conclusion

Retention is affected by many internal and external factors interacting at the individual, group, and organizational levels. This chapter provided an overview of the key factors, challenges, and enablers of military personnel retention based on recent empirical research. While overall CAF attrition is not high, retention of skilled personnel is a perennial concern in single-entry personnel systems because of the costs and limitations related to recruitment, selection, training, and development, along with the significant indirect costs of attrition resulting from loss of expertise, productivity, and workload. Getting and keeping "the right people, with the right skills, in the right place, at the right time" is vital and is a central element of CAF Reconstitution.[76]

Notes

1. Chief of Military Personnel (2009) and Department of National Defence (2017).
2. Goldenberg (2018).
3. Arbour (2022) and Bourgon (2022).
4. Bourgon (2022).
5. Department of National Defence (2017).

6. Canadian Army (2022) and Bourgon (2022).
7. Bourgon (2022, p. 1).
8. Otis and Straver (2008) and NATO Science and Technology Organization (2021).
9. Attrition has been higher in last several years due to increased medical releases, in part due to processing of administrative backlogs. Military Personnel Command (2022) and Straver and Ueno (2018).
10. Straver and Ueno (2018).
11. Boburn and Cowan (2019).
12. Military Personnel Command (2022) and Serré et al. (2016).
13. In recent years, just over 50% of releases of women from the CAF have been for medical reasons. Director Research Workforce Analytics (2018) and Straver and Ueno (2018).
14. Bariteau (2016), King and Goldenberg (2015) and Straver and Arseneau (2019).
15. Golenberg and Laplante (2013) and Previsic et al. (2019).
16. Goldenberg (2018) and Goldenberg and Ben-Ari (2023).
17. Mueller and Straatmann (2014).
18. Meyer and Allen (1991) and Meyer et al. (1993, 2002).
19. Mercurio (2015) and Mueller and Straatmann (2014).
20. Straver and Ueno (2018) and Dale et al. (2020).
21. Manigart et al. (2018) and Office of the Auditor General (2016).
22. Bourgon (2022).
23. Goldenberg (2018).
24. Chief Military Personnel (2009) and Straver and Ueno (2018).
25. Military Personnel Generation (2016, 2022).
26. Goldenberg et al. (2018).
27. Otis and Connick-Keefer (2021).
28. Okros (2016).
29. Goldenberg (2016a), Holton and Fraser (2015), and Okros (2016).
30. Goldenberg (2016b), Okros (2016), and Ouellet (2014).
31. Lee et al. (2022).
32. Anderson (2018).
33. Anderson (2018) and Pearce (2020).
34. Anderson (2018), Pearce (2020) and Yeung et al. (2020).
35. Department of National Defence (2017).
36. Berndtsson et al. (2023).
37. Bariteau (2016).
38. Canadian Armed Forces (2022).
39. Military Personnel Command (2022, p. 2).
40. Ebel-Lam et al. (2018).
41. Ebel-Lam et al. (2018) and Yeung et al. (2020).
42. Military Personnel Generation (2022).

43. Office of the Auditor General (2016); see also House of Commons (2017).
44. Military Personnel Command (2022).
45. Currently there are no set CAF targets for LGBTQ2+ individuals or persons with disabilities.
46. Bourgon (2022).
47. Arbour (2022), CAF Retention Strategy (2022), Davis (2022), Davis and Squires (2019) and Wright et al. (2021).
48. Military Personnel Command (2022) and National Defence (2020, 2021).
49. National Defence (2021).
50. Military Personnel Command (2022).
51. Popov (2011) and Wenek (2012).
52. Department of National Defence (2012, p. 2).
53. Powell-DiSola (2021).
54. Gagné (2017).
55. Department of National Defence (2017).
56. Sudom (2012) and Yeung et al. (2020).
57. Skomorovsky et al. (2022) and Sudom (2012).
58. Chief of Military Personnel (2009, p. 1).
59. Howe (2006) and Goldenberg (2018).
60. Villeneuve et al. (2004).
61. Canadian Armed Forces (2022).
62. Goldenberg (2018).
63. Goldenberg (2018).
64. Dubois (2020).
65. Department of National Defence (2017, p. 69).
66. Chief of Military Personnel (2009) and Goldenberg and Otis (2018).
67. Canadian Armed Forces (2022).
68. Military Personnel Command (2022).
69. Arbour (2022).
70. Chief of Military Personnel (2009) and Military Personnel Command (2022).
71. Military Personnel Command (2022).
72. Military Personnel Command (2022).
73. Goldenberg et al. (2018).
74. Brandes et al. (1999).
75. Colquitt et al. (2001) and Francis and Barling (2005).
76. Bourgon (2022).

REFERENCES

Anderson, Joanna E. 2018. *The 2015 Reserve Force Retention Survey: Descriptive Results for the Primary Reserve*. (Director General Military Personnel Research and Analysis DRDC-RDDC-2017-R162). Ottawa: Defence Research and Development Canada.

Arbour, Louise. 2022. *Report of the Independent External Comprehensive Review of the Department of National Defence and the Canadian Armed Forces*. Montréal: Borden Ladner Gervais.

Bariteau, Col F. 2016. CAF Retention Working Group: Distressed Occupations. Presented to the CAF Retention Working Group.

Berndtsson, Joakim, Irina Goldenberg, and Stéfanie von Hlatky. 2023. *Total Defence Forces in the 21st Century*. Montreal: McGill-Queens University Press.

Boburn, Kelsey, and Allison Cowan. 2019. *Compensation Planning Outlook 2020*. Ottawa: Conference Board of Canada.

Bourgon, MGen Lise. 2022. *CAF Reconstitution—Modernize Military Personnel Management Systems 3350-1* (RTT). Unpublished Departmental Document.

Brandes, P., R. Dharwadkar, and J.W. Dean. 1999. Does Organizational Cynicism Matter? Employee and Supervisor Perspectives on Work Outcomes. *Eastern Academy of Management Best Papers Proceedings* 2 (1): 150–153.

Canadian Armed Forces. 2022. An Interactive Guide for the CAF Offer. Available at http://cmp-cpm.mil.ca/en/support/CAF-Offer.page.

Canadian Armed Forces. 2022. Defence Administrative Orders and Directives (DAOD) 5023-1. Minimum Operational Standards Related to Universality of Service. Available at https://www.canada.ca/en/department-national-defence/corporate/policies-standards/defence-administrative-orders-directives/5000-series/5023/5023-1-minimum-operational-standards-related-to-universality-of-service.html.

Canadian Armed Forces. 2022. Careers. Available at https://forces.ca/en/careers.

Canadian Army 2022. 2022. Canadian Army Reconstitution. Available at https://www.canada.ca/en/army/services/army-narrative/reconstitution/reconstitution.html.

Chief of Military Personnel. 2009. *Military Personnel Retention Strategy* (Technical report 5000-1, CMP). Ottawa: National Defence.

Colquitt, J.A., D.E. Conlon, M.J. Wesson, O.L.H. Porter, and K.Y. Ng. 2001. Justice at the Millennium: A Meta-Analytic Review of 25 Years of Organizational Justice Research. *Journal of Applied Psychology* 86: 425–445. Available at https://doi.org/10.1037//0021-9010.86.3.425.

Dale, A., N. Otis, and M. Boileau. 2020. *Canadian Armed Forces Terms of Service: A Summary of Current Research to Inform Future Use* (Director General Military Personnel Research and Analysis Scientific Letter DRDC-RDDC-2020-L176). Ottawa: Defence Research and Development Canada.

Davis, K.D. 2022. Socio-Cultural Dynamics in Gender and Military Contexts: Seeking and Understanding Change. *Journal of Military, Veteran and Family Health.* Available at doi:https://doi.org/10.3138/jmvfh-2021-0088.

Davis, K.D., and E.C. Squires. 2019. *Culture Shift and Sexual Misconduct: Measurement and Monitoring Strategy* (Director General Military Personnel Research and Analysis Scientific Letter DRDC-RDDC-2019-L335). Ottawa: Defence Research and Development Canada.

Director General Military Personnel. 2018. "Retention Strategy Working Group Presentation." Presented at the CAF Retention Working Group on 30 May, Ottawa, Ontario.

Director Research Workforce Analytics. 2018. *Increasing the Representation of Women in the CAF.* Internal Unpublished Presentation.

Dubois, Col Stefan. 2020. *Adaptive Career Path Bi-Monthly Director Meeting / CCA reunion bi mensuelle des directeurs.* Director of Personnel Plans / Directeur des Plan du Personnel. Director General Military Personnel Strategy. April.

Ebel-Lam, A., J. Anderson, and N. Otis. 2018. *Factors Affecting the Recruitment and Retention of Medical Officers in the Canadian Armed Forces: A Mixed-Method Analysis* (Director General Military Personnel Research and Analysis DRDC-RDDC-2018-R174). Ottawa, ON: Defence Research and Development Canada.

Francis, L., and J. Barling. 2005. Organizational Injustice and Psychological Strain. *Canadian Journal of Behavioural Science/Revue canadienne des sciences du comportement* 37: 250–261. Available at https://doi.org/10.1037/h0087260.

Gagné, Maj L. H. 2017. *Separation of Married Service Couples: Problem or Part of Military Life?* Canadian Forces College, JCSP 43—PCEMI 43. Kingston, ON: Canadian Forces College.

Goldenberg, Irina. 2016a. *Harnessing the 21st Century Competencies Project—Implications for Key Human Resources Functions* (Director General Military Personnel Research and Analysis DRDC-RDDC-2016-B003 DTN 7258). Ottawa, ON: Defence Research and Development Canada.

Goldenberg, Irina. 2016b. *Harnessing the 21st Century Competencies Project—Post-millennial Cohort Characteristics* (Director General Military Personnel Research and Analysis DRDC-RDDC-2016-B002; DTN 7252). Ottawa, ON: Defence Research and Development Canada.

Goldenberg, Irina. 2018. *Building a Culture of Retention in the Armed Forces.* The European Defence Agency—Cap Tech 4 Meeting—21 February 2018. Brussels, Belgium.

Goldenberg, Irina, and Ben-Ari Eyal. 2023. Transmigration, Voluntary Service and Complementary Careers: A Comparison of Canadian Regular and Reserve

Force Military Members. In *Contemporary Military Reserves*, ed. Eyal Ben-Ari and Vincent Connelly, 39–61. Routledge.

Goldenberg, Irina, and J. Laplante. 2013. *CAF Retention Survey, Army Attrition Monitoring Program Questionnaire, and CAF Exit Survey Analyses for Land Force Western Area* (Director General Military Personnel Research and Analysis DRDC-RDDC-2013-6600 to LFWA COMD and DGLS/COS Land Ops).

Goldenberg, Irina, and Nancy Otis. 2018. *Occupational Choice: Sex Comparisons in Recruitment and Early Retention Research.* Briefing Note to Commander Military Personnel Command.

Goldenberg, Irina, Nancy Otis, J. Laplante, and S. Pearce. 2018. *Positive Aspects of Basic Training and Suggestions for Improvement: Phase 2 Qualitative Findings* (Director General Military Personnel Research and Analysis DRDC-RDDC-2018-L178). Ottawa: Defence Research and Development Canada.

Government of Canada, Department of National Defence. 2012. *Director Military Careers Standard Operation Procedures—Posting Married Service Couples.* Ottawa: Department of National Defence.

Government of Canada, Department of National Defence. 2017. Strong, Secure, Engaged: Canada's Defence Policy. Available at https://www.canada.ca/en/department-national-defence/corporate/reports-publications/canada-defence-policy.html/.

Government of Canada, Department of National Defence. 2020. *The Path to Dignity and Respect: The Canadian Armed Forces Sexual Misconduct Response Strategy.* Ottawa: National Defence.

Government of Canada, Department of National Defence. 2021. CDS/DM Initiating Directive for Professional Conduct and Culture. Available at https://www.canada.ca/en/department-national-defence/corporate/policies-standards/dm-cds-directives/cds-dm-initiating-directive-professional-conduct-culture.html.

Holton, T., and B. Fraser. 2015. *Generation Z and Technology: Constructing Tomorrow's Boundary Spanners* (Director General Military Personnel Research and Analysis DRDC-RDDC-2015-R167). Ottawa: Defence Research and Development Canada.

House of Commons. 2017. Report 5, Canadian Armed Forces Recruitment and Retention—National Defence, of the Fall 2016 Reports of the Auditor General of Canada. Report of the Standing Committee on Public Accounts. June 2017. Ottawa: Parliament of Canada.

Howe, D. 2006. *Building and Sustaining a Retention Culture in the Canadian Forces* (DPGR A/RT Report 2006-006). Ottawa: Defence Research and Development Canada.

King, C., and Irina Goldenberg. 2015. Personnel Retention and Distressed Trades. Briefing to the CAF Retention Working Group, Presented at First Meeting of the CAF Retention Working Group. Ottawa.

Lee, J.E.C., Irina Goldenberg, A.-R. Blais, C. Comeau, C. Daugherty, E. Guérin, C. Frank, M. M. LeBlanc, J. Peach, K. Pearce, K. Sudom, and Z. Wang. 2022. Trials and Tribulations Among Members of Canada's Defence Team Early in the Pandemic: Key Insights from the COVID-19 Defence Team Survey. *Health Promotion and Chronic Disease Prevention in Canada: Research, Policy and Practice/HPCDP Journal* 42 (3): 104–112. Available at https://doi.org/10.24095/hpcdp.42.3.04.

Manigart, Philippe, Tessa op den Buijs, Erik van Doorn, Emma Jonsson, Valerian Lecoq, Rene Moelker, Johan Österberg, Nancy Otis, Frank Brundtland Steder, and Tibor Szvircsev Tresch. 2018. *The Impact of Demographic Change on Recruitment and Retention of Personnel in European Armed Forces: Final Report Opinions of Young Prospects and International Experts.* Brussels: European Defence Agency.

Mercurio, Zachary A. 2015. Affective Commitment as a Core Essence of Organizational Commitment: An Integrative Literature Review. *Human Resource Development Review* 14 (4): 389–414. Available at https://doi.org/10.1177/1534484315603612.

Meyer, John P., and Natalie J Allen. 1991. A Three-Component Conceptualization of Organizational Commitment. *Human Resource Management Review* 1 (1): 61–89. Available at https://doi.org/10.1016/1053-4822(91)90011-Z.

Meyer, John P., Natalie J. Allen, and Catherine A. Smith. 1993. Commitment to Organizations and Occupations: Extension and Test of a Three-Component Conceptualization. *Journal of Applied Psychology* 78 (4): 538–551. Available at https://doi.org/10.1037/0021-9010.78.4.538.

Meyer, John P., David J. Stanley, Lynne Herscovitch, and Laryssa Topolnytsky. 2002. Affective, Continuance, and Normative Commitment to the Organization: A Meta-Analysis of Antecedents, Correlates, and Consequences. *Journal of Vocational Behavior* 61 (1): 20–52. Available at https://doi.org/10.1006/jvbe.2001.1842.

Military Personnel Command. 2022. *CAF Retention Strategy* [Draft]. Ottawa: National Defence.

Military Personnel Generation. 2016. R3 Brief: Optimizing Requirements, Recruiting, and Retention Systems. Presentation to the CAF Retention Working Group, Ottawa.

Military Personnel Generation. 2022. Annual Military Occupation Review/Strategic Intake Plan. Presentation to Director Personnel Generation Requirements, Ottawa.

Mueller, K., and T. Straatmann. 2014. Organizational Commitment. In *Encyclopedia of Quality of Life and Well-Being Research,* ed. A.C. Michalos,

4520–4525. Dordrecht: Springer. Available at https://doi.org/10.1007/978-94-007-0753-5_2030.

NATO Science and Technology Organization. 2021. Retention in the Armed Forces—Technical Activity Proposal of the Human Factors and Medicine Panel. Unpublished Document.

Office of the Auditor General of Canada. 2016. *Report 5—Canadian Armed Forces Recruitment and Retention—National Defence*. Available at http://www.oag-bvg.gc.ca/internet/English/parl_oag_201611_05_e_41834.html.

Okros, A. 2016. *Harnessing the 21st Century Competencies* (Director General Military Personnel Research and Analysis Contract Report). Ottawa: Director General Military Personnel Research and Analysis, 2015.

Otis, Nancy, and S.J. Connick-Keefer. 2021. *Qualitative Analysis of Recruits' Unmet or Surpassed Expectations About Basic Training* (Director General Military Personnel Research and Analysis Scientific Report, DRDC-RDDC-2021-R132). Ottawa: Defence Research and Development Canada.

Otis, Nancy, and M. Staver. 2008. *Review of Attrition and Retention for the Canadian Forces* (Director General Military Personnel Research and Analysis TM 2008-30). Ottawa: Director General Military Personnel Research and Analysis, Department of National Defence.

Ouellet, E. 2014. Assessment of Canadian Armed Forces' Institutional Perception of Youth through Symbolic Representations, 2000-Present. Paper presented at the 2014 Biennial Conference of the Inter-University Seminar on the Armed Forces and Society (Canada), Ottawa 17–19 October.

Pearce, Sean. 2020. *The 2019 Primary Reserve Force Retention Survey* (Director General Military Personnel Research and Analysis DRDC-RDDC-2020-R038). Ottawa: Defence Research and Development Canada.

Popov, M.N. 2011. *A Thousand Paper Cuts—Canadian Forces Attrition, Retention, and the Confluence of Factors that Influence Our People*. Canadian Forces College, JCSP 37. Kingston: Canadian Forces College.

Powell-DiSola, Leila. 2021. *Coping Strategies and Relationship Satisfaction Among Dual-Military Married Army Couples*. Walden Dissertations and Doctoral Studies, no. 10835. Available at https://scholarworks.waldenu.edu/dissertations/10835.

Previsic, Ivana, Anna Ebel-Lam, and Irina Goldenberg. 2019. *4 Wing Cold Lake Retention Study: A Mixed-Method Analysis* (Director General Military Personnel Research and Analysis DRDC-RDDC-2019-R105). Ottawa: Defence Research and Development Canada.

Serré, L., Irina Goldenberg, and Nancy Otis. 2016. *Annual Report on Regular Force Attrition 2014/2015* (Director General Military Personnel Research and Analysis DRDC-RDDC-2016-R7450; DTN 7450). Ottawa, ON: Defence Research and Development Canada.

Skomorovsky, A., J.A. Chamberland, and C. Wan. 2022. Spousal Psychological Health: The Roles of Military Spouse Health and Protective Factors. *Journal of Military, Veteran, and Family Health*, Special Issue on Resilience of Canadian Military Families.

Straver, Michelle, and L. Arseneau. 2019. *Analysis of Occupations Experiencing Shortages. Contribution to North Atlantic Treaty Organization System Analysis and Studies-128 Activity* (Director General Military Personnel Research and Analysis DRDC-RDDC-2019-D090). Ottawa: Defence Research and Development Canada.

Straver, Michelle, and Ryuichi Ueno. 2018. Overview of Regular Force Attrition. Presented to Retention Strategy Working Group, May. Ottawa.

Sudom, K. 2012. *Impact of Military Life on Families and Single Canadian Forces Members: Current State of Knowledge and Research Gaps* (Director General Military Personnel Research and Analysis Technical Memorandum 2012-008). Ottawa: Defence Research and Development Canada.

Villeneuve, M., T. Dobreva-Martinova, and J.G. Currie. 2004. *Buying Low Attrition or Building High Retention? That Is the Question*, DMEP-A/RT Report 2004-06. Ottawa: Department of National Defence.

Wenek, K. 2012. Personnel Research and Military Personnel Policy. Personnel Research Symposium Keynote Address (by DGMP). Ottawa.

Wright, J., B. Waruszynski, S. Sillins, and V. Giroux-Lalonde. 2021. Systemic Racism and Discrimination in the Canadian Armed Forces (Director General Military Personnel Research and Analysis DRDC-RDDC-2021-D121). Ottawa: Defence Research and Development Canada.

Yeung, Edward, Evanya Musolino, and Emrah Eren. 2020. *The 2019 CAF Regular Force Retention Survey: Descriptive Statistics* (Director General Military Personnel Research and Analysis DRDC-RDDC-2020-C016). Ottawa: Defence Research and Development Canada.

Climate Insecurity and Canadian Defence

Wilfrid Greaves

It is an urgent fact and a banal trope that Earth's climate is growing warmer and less predictable due to human activity. The global rate of natural and human-caused greenhouse gas emissions (GHGs) exceeds any period in the last 22,000 years; GHG concentrations in the atmosphere are higher than they have been for 800,000 years, and the planet is on track to exceed the worst-case climate scenarios modelled by the United Nations Intergovernmental Panel on Climate Change.[1] This has raised scientific concern over ecological "tipping points" that may catalyse catastrophic harm to ecological systems and human and non-human resilience around the globe, such as rapid sea level rise, trophic cascades, disrupted oceanic heat circulation, and biodiversity collapse.[2] This new geological era of the Anthropocene, characterized by human interference in Earth's systems on a planetary scale, is undermining Earth's capacity to provide a "safe operating space for humanity," leading scientists to note the growing difficulty for humanity to avoid a "ghastly future."[3] The United Nations Secretary-General has issued dire warnings of climate

---

W. Greaves (✉)
Department of Political Science, University of Victoria, Victoria, BC, Canada
e-mail: wgreaves@uvic.ca

© The Author(s), under exclusive license to Springer Nature Switzerland AG 2023
T. Juneau and P. Lagassé (eds.), *Canadian Defence Policy in Theory and Practice, Volume 2*, Canada and International Affairs, https://doi.org/10.1007/978-3-031-37542-2_4

change as the gravest threat to international peace and security, and the UN Development Programme notes that "the unprecedented context of the Anthropocene is the backdrop for a new generation of threats that are global, systemic and interlinked."[4] Regrettably, sufficiently rapid global reductions of GHGs to keep average temperatures below 2 °C are unlikely, and climate change will worsen over the coming century.

As one of the largest and most ecologically diverse countries in the world, Canada is extremely vulnerable to the effects of climate change. Its high latitude and the susceptibility of Arctic and sub-Arctic ecosystems to climate change mean that Canada has already warmed by approximately twice the global average, with many communities experiencing severe climate-related damage. Its massive land area; diversity of climate regions, ecosystems, and species; expansive and vulnerable infrastructure; and a population that, on the one hand, is clustered in dense urban areas and, on the other, scattered in isolated rural communities, pose a range of climate vulnerabilities. The federal government's 2019 climate change assessment outlined the most significant impacts, including ocean acidification, wildfires, increased but less predictable precipitation, flooding, drought, blizzards, heatwaves, hurricanes, tornados, coastal erosion, and permafrost thaw.[5] These affect Canadian security and defence in various ways, including the production of new conventional and unconventional threats to Canada's national interests and the increased operational tempo of the Canadian Armed Forces (CAF) in responding to domestic climate-related emergencies.

Given its world-leading (with Australia) per capita GHG emissions and its role as one of the largest hydrocarbon producers in the world, Canada is directly implicated in the historical and contemporary causes of climate change, namely large-scale land use and the industrialized burning of carbon-based energy for transportation, electricity, and heat. Hydrocarbons have become a central, but divisive, part of Canada's economy and dominant national identity since the mid-twentieth century, reflected most acutely in the contentious national debates over expanding Canada's oil and gas exports in the twenty-first century.[6] Though a participant in the global climate change regime since its inception in 1992, Canada has been widely criticized for advocating for reduced international ambition and as a laggard in meeting its own emissions reduction targets.[7] Although significant climate change policies have been implemented under the current Liberal government—notably the federal price on carbon, emissions intensity targets for oil and gas, and measures to limit oil and gas shipping off the west coast—oil and gas remain Canada's largest exports, and direct and indirect fossil fuel-related activities comprise approximately 10% of national GDP. Canada's relationship to the causes and effects of climate change thus remains complex, fraught, and deeply conflicted.

This chapter outlines the connections between climate change, defence, and security in Canada. First, it reviews the scholarship on security and the natural environment, including the limited research examining climate change as an issue for Canadian security and defence. It then examines how climate change has been incorporated into Canadian defence and security policy. These two sections emphasize a similar pattern: when included in defence and security analysis, climate change is generally framed as a foreign issue in the Global South and a regional issue in the circumpolar Arctic. Such accounts reproduce a misunderstanding of climate change as principally a security threat in the Global South and the circumpolar Arctic, obscuring the broader salience of climate change for the security of privileged regions and populations across the Global North, including southern Canada. The chapter outlines how climate change affects three areas of Canadian security and defence: destabilizing the international security environment; more frequent domestic emergencies; and the need to "green" national defence to reduce the environmental impact of the Canadian Armed Forces. It concludes by stressing the need for Canadian politics to allow the CAF and other defence and security organs of the Canadian state to better and more consistently prepare for a climate-disrupted future.

Studying Canadian Defence, Security, and Climate Change

Though analytically distinct, the concepts of defence and security became entangled during the post-World War II period. Defence denotes the protection of a state's territory, population, and core national interests against external, principally military, threats. This is normally, though not always, achieved through a state's own military capabilities. By contrast, security classically refers to the condition of a person feeling at ease in the expectation of their physical safety and social well-being.[8] Security was thus originally conceived as an individual trait, but over time evolved into a collective property of a community or society. Including the national population among the objects to be defended through military force brought the provision of security, so defined, into the framework of national defence. Eventually, the two concepts became closely linked, with the protection of the sovereign state and the people within its borders merging into the powerful twentieth-century signifier of "national security." Encompassing both military and non-military threats, national security was conceptually dominant, indeed nearly hegemonic, in the field of security and defence studies from the early years of the Cold War onward.[9]

Security also has connotations that transcend the apparent simplicity of defining national defence in military terms or national security in military terms.[10] Security was the subject of hot debate in the 1980s and 1990s as the impending end of the Cold War and illusory hopes for a peace dividend opened space for conceptual and theoretical efforts to "redefine security."[11] Pointing to the generation of new phenomena, structures, and processes as a result of economic globalization, technological modernization, and the diffusion of social and political power to new actors, critical security scholars insisted on a range of harms and dangers excluded by statist conceptions of national defence. Some, including Canadians Keith Krause and Michael C. Williams, called for the broadening and deepening of security to include non-military threats (broadening) to objects above and below the state (deepening), while noting the underlying epistemological debates over whether the nature of security threats is objective, subjective, or socially constructed.[12]

Two features of these wide-ranging debates in security studies and International Relations are relevant to climate change and defence in the Canadian context. First, the military defence of territory, population, and national interests has never captured the reality of defence in Canada. As Kim Richard Nossal explains, "Canadian defence policy can only be understood when it is conceived as a policy designed to defend something more than just Canadian territorial integrity and the security and well-being of Canadians."[13] At different points in its history since 1867, Canada's military or para-military capabilities have been applied to various goals, such as opening the Prairies to colonial settlement, participating in foreign military expeditions alongside other British imperial forces, and deploying to Europe and Asia to defend allied democracies against authoritarian aggression during both world wars and the Cold War. But, as Stephanie Carvin notes, "surrounded by three oceans and with a (mostly) benevolent neighbour to our south, Canada has not faced a realistic threat of imminent invasion since the mid-nineteenth century."[14] Ironically, this risk of invasion was at the hands of the United States, which since the 1870s has become Canada's closest, though not always constant, military ally and national security partner.[15] As a result, one perennial debate has been whether the goals of Canadian defence policy include defending against unwelcome American help in protecting the northern half of North America.[16] Regardless, since the primary objective of Canadian defence policy has never really been the direct defence of its territory from foreign aggression, studies of Canadian defence have, perhaps, allowed a wider examination of national security interests than states with less favourable geostrategic circumstances.

Second, the late- and post-Cold War debates over broadening the meaning of security were directly fuelled by emerging awareness of the global ecological crisis. "Environmental security" was the most important wedge in the door of traditional security studies' narrow focus on the threat and use of military force. This drew first on earlier work examining environmental threats to states' core national interests, then on research identifying causal relationships between environmental stresses and violent conflict, including the pioneering scholarship of another Canadian, Thomas Homer-Dixon.[17] Writing in the mid-1990s, Krause and Williams concluded that "perhaps the most widespread call to redefine security has emerged from the claim that environmental degradation poses a threat to the ecosystem or to human well-being that transcends particular states and conceptions of national security."[18] Since then, the volume of research exploring the multi-causal relationships between environmental change, armed conflict, and human insecurity has grown as understanding of global ecological change has improved.[19]

However, despite widespread recognition that climate change exacerbates existing security challenges and generates new threats, there has been limited research into the security and defence implications of climate change for Canada. Writing in 2010, Leanne Purdy and Margaret Smythe noted that although Canada hosted the first international conference on climate change in 1988, "since that ground-breaking event, the climate change-security nexus has not been discussed, debated, or analyzed in any serious, sustained, or comprehensive way in Canada."[20] A 2012 report outlined climate-related human security threats to vulnerable populations in Canada and reiterated the lack of appropriate policy responses.[21] Little was written over the following decade, but 2021 marked a renewed interest in climate and security in Canada. The CIGI think tank released a report echoing previous conclusions that climate change threatens public safety, vulnerable peoples, and the Arctic and noted that Canada must expand its capabilities to adequately respond.[22] DND funded a report by a U.S. think tank that assessed climate-related threats to Canada domestically, within North America, and internationally, and called for creation of a Climate Security Task Force to coordinate and plan for future climate-related security challenges.[23] For his part, in one article Greaves identified five climate-related security threats to Canada: human insecurity, economic threats, Arctic threats, humanitarian crises, and increased domestic conflict, and in another examined how Canada's contentious domestic climate politics prevent the effective treatment of climate change as a security issue.[24]

Some recent climate security research examines the implications for CAF operations, but most focuses on the human and environmental security dimensions of climate change, with limited application to national defence. For instance, in a 2014 study, Greaves outlined a heterogeneous field of critical environmental security scholarship in Canada characterized by five overlapping sets of security issues: climate change; industry, natural resource extraction, and pollution; the lived insecurities of Indigenous peoples and other non-dominant groups; the Arctic region; and retheorizing the links between the environment, violence, and social conflict.[25] In a more recent analysis of articles published in five relevant journals between 1989 and 2022, Greaves and Gricius showed that climate change has been substantively marginal to the fields of Canadian political science, foreign policy analysis, and security and defence.[26] We concluded that Canadian foreign, security, and defence scholarship tends to omit climate change except in the context of Northern Canada and the circumpolar Arctic.

The Arctic looms large in discourses of climate change and security in Canada. Climate change has contributed to concerns over increasingly competitive inter-state behaviour that will challenge Canada's ability to defend its Arctic interests.[27] The risk of inter-state conflict spilling into the Arctic has been a serious concern since Russia invaded and annexed the Ukrainian territory of Crimea in 2014, but relations descended to a new low after Russia's expanded invasion of Ukraine in early 2022. Although all Arctic states still affirm their commitment to peaceful resolution of regional disputes, the new geopolitical reality of an Arctic partitioned between Western and Russian zones engaged in a high stakes conflict in Ukraine raises tensions in the region.[28] Although not caused by climate change, the deterioration of Arctic relations due to Russia's war against

Ukraine compounds 15 years of rhetoric about growing climate-related competition due to the increased navigability of Arctic waters and greater accessibility of Arctic resources.[29] As a leading Arctic state defensive of its territorial claims and among the most bellicose towards Russia, Canada is deeply implicated in these intersecting discourses of Arctic climate change, natural resources, and regional security competition.[30]

The CAF is one of the lead federal agencies in the Canadian Arctic,[31] and climate change is an implicit theme of Arctic defence research nominally focused on military procurement, the changing international security environment, and the asymmetrical partnership with the United States.[32] The Arctic showcases unique implications of climate change for security by aggravating existing security threats and creating new ones, such as the anticipated opening of Canada's Arctic waters, including the Northwest Passage, to increased marine traffic.[33] Climate-related Arctic security issues include unconventional threats such as illegal shipping, smuggling, oil spills, search and rescue, irregular migration, and other criminal activities.[34] While there is no evidence a warming environment will directly cause inter-state violence in the Arctic, climate change is producing an increasingly complex regional security environment characterized by renewed inter-state competition, the pursuit of economic gains, and sustained ecological and social harms. In this context, there is an important role for the CAF in providing security in the Arctic that includes but extends beyond national defence.

Governing Canadian Defence, Security, and Climate Change

Climate change has not been considered relevant to national security and defence in Canada until recently and, even then, incompletely. Since 2015, the federal government has demonstrated more commitment to addressing the impacts of climate change across departments.[35] Many of the Trudeau Government's mandate letters to Cabinet ministers refer to climate change, with a particular focus on the Arctic.[36] However, limited attention is paid to the implications of climate change for defence and security and, when it is, it typically frames these as external to Canada and the security of (most) Canadians. Government documents that discuss climate and security remain mostly descriptive of climate impacts, rather than detailing military or government preparedness and responses.

For example, neither of Canada's two most recent defence strategies meaningfully addresses climate change. The Harper Government's 2008 *Canada First Defence Strategy* does not mention climate change once, alluding instead to "changing weather patterns" in the Arctic.[37] The Trudeau Government's 2017 *Strong, Secure, Engaged* (SSE) specifies that climate change must be considered through a security lens, but does not incorporate it further into its analysis of Canadian interests. SSE frames the implications of climate change for security in two ways. First, it will aggravate existing international vulnerabilities such as weak governance, worsen sources of tension such as resource scarcity, and is already generating humanitarian crises that produce demands for external intervention.[38] Second, SSE focuses on the Arctic, specifying that climate-related safety and security challenges in Northern Canada include greater demand for search and rescue and the need to defend against hostile foreign activities. However, it takes a broad and descriptive approach to climate change throughout and outlines no new tools or actions. By describing climate change as a "security challenge that knows no borders"[39] but focusing on international and Arctic security threats related to climate change, SSE implies that climate change principally affects security in Northern Canada or distant, developing regions of the world.

It shares this perspective with Canada's 2019 *Arctic and Northern Policy Framework*, which under the heading "safety, security and defence" notes that "questions around environmental protection and response, safe regional transportation, and search and rescue capabilities were raised as critical issues, especially in the context of a rapidly changing climate."[40] Analytically linking threats and vulnerabilities in the Global South to the "Fourth World" of small, remote communities in Northern Canada with similarly inadequate infrastructure, limited public services, and lack of financing for suitable adaptation demonstrates that climate-related insecurities are unevenly distributed according to existing social inequalities, power hierarchies, and access to various forms of capital.[41] This explains the analytical focus on these two regions, and also why discussing human security in the Arctic has been a double-edged sword for Canada due to its own culpability in contributing to and ultimately failing to defend against the threats posed by climate change to some of the most vulnerable people in the country.[42]

There are indications that climate change is being taken more seriously by Canadian security and defence planners. A 2021 analysis by the Canadian Security Intelligence Service (CSIS) lists ten "climate security factors" in Canada across a wide array of dimensions: Arctic, border, coastal, domestic, energy, health, food, and water security, as well as "financial capacity" to adapt to climate impacts, and what the report calls a "security accelerant," akin to the concept of climate threat as a threat multiplier employed by states and actors such as the U.S. military.[43] CSIS summarizes that, "put simply, climate change compounds all other known human security issues and serves as an accelerant towards negative security outcomes [...] There will be no single moment where this threat will crystallize and reveal itself, for it is already underway and will incrementally build across decades to come."[44] Though not reflected in policy, this assessment suggests an increasingly sophisticated federal engagement with the security dimensions of climate change. Canada is also establishing a new NATO Climate and Security Centre of Excellence (CASCOE), to be based in Montréal starting in 2023. CASCOE is expected to help coordinate improved climate and security planning, assessing operational considerations, and developing best practices to reduce NATO militaries' contributions to atmospheric greenhouse gas emissions. Nonetheless, overall, there has been limited or conflicted policy action towards addressing climate change as a security issue in Canada.

Climate Change and Canadian Defence

Three primary areas of Canadian security and defence policy involving the CAF are affected by climate change: it destabilizes the international security environment; increases climate-related domestic emergencies; and requires the "greening" of national defence to reduce the CAF's environmental impact. Internationally, climate change worsens existing human security challenges, creates new ones, and contributes to underlying causes of large-scale group and inter-state conflict. Though not the "resource wars" of earlier geopolitical imaginings, climate change further strains already fragile social, political, and economic systems; contributes to natural resource scarcity, poverty, and hunger; and worsens environmental degradation, including eroding the ecological services that underpin human life and flourishing.[45] Particularly concerning are the effects on food and water availability, with extreme temperatures and more frequent and severe droughts raising the probability of conflicts in countries already experiencing resource scarcity. In turn, conflicts in climate-stressed regions can undermine state capacity in ways that fuel international instability.[46] While there has been debate over the causal relationship between climate change and particular armed conflicts, evidence for climate-related conflict links in regions like the African Sahel appears more robust.[47] Canadian and NATO allied troops have participated in recent multilateral military operations across North Africa and the Middle East, and the frequency and intensity of social unrest that can fuel conflict is likely to increase due to climate-related impacts.

In addition to armed conflicts, extreme weather events will produce humanitarian crises that Canada may be called to respond to. In past crises, Canada deployed the Disaster Assistance Response Team (DART), a military unit tasked with rapid response to relieve humanitarian suffering in the wake of environmental disasters. DART performed well during its seven international deployments between its establishment in 1998 and 2015, though it has not been deployed under the current Liberal government.[48] Humanitarian need will also accompany the rise of climate-related migration. Already the world has a record 250 million displaced people, with another 200 million predicted to be displaced by climate change by 2050.[49] Most will not reach Canada but will require aid and resources, and their management will further strain international institutions. All told, "these scenarios prompt questions about the coping capacity of international security institutions, the preparedness of humanitarian mechanisms, the protection of refugees, and the responses of countries such as Canada to catastrophic situations around the world at a time when specialized resources may be stretched as a result of climate change-induced situations at home."[50] The need to respond to climate-related humanitarian crises will increase at the same time that climate change will increasingly batter the global economy and strain state capacities to respond.

At the same time, climate change is increasing domestic demand for the CAF to respond to more frequent emergencies as a result of extreme weather events.[51] Operation LENTUS, the standing framework through which civilian authorities request CAF assistance in responding to natural disasters, was activated at least 38 times with increasing frequency between 2010 and 2022: 12 deployments between 2010 and 2016, compared to 26 between 2018 and 2022.[52] In 2021 alone there were seven LENTUS deployments in four provinces and two territories, including hundreds of personnel deployed to prepare and assist with flooding in Yukon and B.C., wildfires in B.C., Ontario, and Manitoba, flooding in Newfoundland, and to provide potable water for Iqaluit, Nunavut after thawing permafrost caused diesel contamination of the municipal water system. The scale of these operations is often modest, but can be significant, such as the more than 2,300 CAF personnel who deployed to combat floods in southern Alberta in 2013. During the COVID-19 pandemic, hundreds more CAF members supported the federal government's response by distributing vaccines and supporting other public health measures through Operations LASER and VECTOR, including assisting in long-term care homes in Ontario and Québec. Given that climate change also increases the likelihood of future viral pandemics,[53] the CAF's logistical expertise and emergency response capabilities will likely face increased strain in the coming years as responses to climate-related challenges all draw on the same limited pool of military resources.

In 2019, the then-Chief of the Defence Staff (CDS) noted that "these calls for assistance are stretching the military beyond what it was originally designed to handle," and that the CAF is "probably too small to be able to deal with all of the tasks."[54] The current CDS made similar statements in 2020 while commander of the Army: "If this becomes of a larger scale, more frequent basis, it will start to affect [the CAF's] readiness" for combat operations.[55] These warnings have led to calls for Canada to establish a civilian entity to act as the first responder in domestic emergencies, which would allow the CAF to retain its core focus on national defence.[56] Similar calls have been made to expand the role of the Canadian Rangers to serve as first responders for search and rescue (SAR) and other local emergencies in rural, remote, and Northern communities, reducing their reliance on SAR capabilities based far to the south.[57] Without such changes, the primary role and culture of the CAF in the future may no longer be preparing for overseas expeditionary combat, but for domestic operations in response to climate change.

Finally, the connections between climate change and Canadian defence include the need to reduce the carbon emissions of defence activities. Canada's international commitment is to reduce its GHG emissions by 40–45% below 2005 levels by 2030 and to reach net-zero emissions nationally and in Government of Canada operations by 2050. DND and the CAF represent nearly 60% of the Government of Canada's total GHG emissions, making defence reductions in the areas of DND-owned and -leased real estate, vehicle fleets and travel, procurement, and national safety and security operations necessary for Canada to reach its overall targets.[58]

To achieve these goals, the *Defence Energy and Environment Strategy* (DEES) was released for 2017–2020 and renewed for 2020–2023. Its objectives include greening national defence in three distinct ways: reducing energy waste and using lower-carbon energy sources; reducing climate change risks to defence programmes, operations, and infrastructure; and reducing the defence impacts on the natural environment from infrastructure, vehicles and aircraft, and equipment.[59] DND GHG emissions reduction measures include new and upgraded defence buildings to meet the latest industry standards for excellence in green building design, construction, and maintenance; shifting electricity used on bases and other military facilities to low-carbon sources; and transitioning the military's light-duty vehicle fleet to hybrid or electric technology.[60] In its 2021–2022 DEES results report, DND indicated it had achieved 75% clean energy on its bases and facilities, and a 36% emissions reduction for its buildings and commercial light-duty vehicle fleet, and was on track to reach the 40% reduction target by 2030 and 80% by 2050.[61] This indicates substantial progress towards curbing the GHG emissions of Canada's military.

However, significant challenges remain in reducing DND and the CAF's carbon footprint, including "very significant gaps in [emissions] reporting."[62] Canada's "national safety and security operations" are currently exempt from emissions reduction targets, meaning that the full scope of DND's contributions to Canada's aggregate GHGs is not captured by current data. However, by end of 2023 national safety and security departments including DND, CAF, the Coast Guard, and the Royal Canadian Mounted Police are mandated to develop decarbonization plans to align their emission reduction pathways with the 2050 net-zero target. Fuel use by the Royal Canadian Air Force and Royal Canadian Navy are of particular concern, accounting for 81% and 18% respectively of DND's national safety and security emissions, and more than two thirds of Canada's national safety and security emissions.[63] This highlights the need to consider the operational feasibility of low-carbon fuel sources, as well as more efficient flight operations, use of flight simulators, sustainable aviation fuels, and solar-powered aircraft and airships.[64] Such efforts to reduce GHG emissions are key methods by which DND and the CAF can contribute to combatting climate change.

Conclusion

Despite increasingly severe impacts across the country, Canadian security and defence policy does not reflect the seriousness of climate change. Writing in 2010, Purdy and Smythe observed that "Canada's security players seem disconnected from – and disinterested in – the findings and insights of climate experts."[65] More than a decade later, government and public attention on climate change have increased, but it remains only shallowly incorporated into defence planning. Though research on the climate security nexus has grown, it remains limited and isolated from mainstream scholarship on Canadian defence, security, and foreign policy. This is despite the evident threats climate change poses to Canada and Canadians, whether categorized as public safety, national security, and international security threats, or human security, economic threats, Arctic threats, humanitarian crises, and risks of domestic conflict.[66] Climate change is already affecting Canada's security and defence interests by destabilizing the international security environment, increasing domestic demands for disaster preparedness and emergency response, and necessitating the decarbonization of defence and national security activities to meet Canada's international climate obligations.

While addressing climate change has been championed by the current government, it remains framed principally as a political and economic issue rather than one of national security or defence. Although a whole-of-government approach to climate change is necessary, the limited securitization of climate change is due to the basic realities of Canadian politics: federalism, partisanship, and the contentious regional politics of emissions reduction and fossil fuel extraction.[67] In this respect, it is not an issue solely that defence policymakers or military leaders can resolve. The political contestation around climate change policy in Canada, particularly by conservative political parties, affects national defence, not least when incorporating climate change into national defence priorities is met by critique of the CAF as fighting a flank in a progressive-conservative culture war.[68] Such politicization is manifestly counterproductive to the national interest and national defence, which demand evidence-based analysis of the security and defence implications of climate change, not reactionary nostalgia. As Canada haltingly prepares for a climate changed-future, national defence will require a sustained and costly commitment to both climate change adaptation and mitigation. It remains to be seen whether current levels of political and strategic commitment to incorporating climate change into defence and security planning will be adequate to the defence of the nation and its interests, or whether such commitment will survive the next federal change of government. Alas, such political uncertainty is likely to make it harder to defend Canada and Canadians from the effects of a changing climate that does not care how much we try to wish it away.

Notes

1. Intergovernmental Panel on Climate Change (2022).
2. Lenton et al. (2008), Lenton (2012) and Fewster et al. (2022).
3. Bradshaw et al. (2021), Crutzen (2002), Rockström et al. (2009) and Potsdam Institute for Climate Impact Research and Climate Analytics (2013).
4. United Nations Development Programme (2022, p. 21) and United Nations (n.d.).
5. Bush and Lemmen (2019).
6. Preston (2017), Boyd (2019) and Anderson and Coletto (2017).
7. Winfield et al. (2022).
8. Rothschild (1995).
9. Wolfers (1952) and Buzan and Hansen (2009).
10. Walt (1991).
11. Brown (1977), Ullman (1983), Renner (1989) and Mathews (1989).
12. Krause and Williams (1996) and Smith (2005).
13. Nossal (2004, p. 504).
14. Carvin (2021, p. 6).
15. Greaves (2020), Keeble (2005) and Lennox (2007).
16. Barry and Bratt (2008) and Lagassé (2010).
17. Homer-Dixon (1991, 1994, 1999) and Homer-Dixon and Blitt (1998).
18. Krause and Williams (1996, p. 233).
19. See, for example, Jon Barnett, *The Meaning of Environmental Security: Ecological Politics and Policy in the New Security Era* (London: Zed Books, 2001); Simon Dalby, *Environmental security* (Minneapolis: University of Minnesota Press, 2002); Simon Dalby, *Security and environmental change* (Cambridge: Polity, 2009); Daniel H. Deudney and Richard A. Matthew, eds, *Contested Grounds: Security and Conflict in the New Environmental Politics* (Albany: SUNY Press, 1999); Rita Floyd and Richard A. Matthew, *Environmental Security: Approaches and Issues* (New York: Routledge, 2013); Cameron Harrington and Clifford Shearing, *Security in the Anthropocene: Reflections on Safety and Care* (New York: Columbia University Press, 2017).

20. Purdy and Smythe (2010, p. 411).
21. McBean et al. (2021).
22. Dalby and Lawrence (2021).
23. Conger and Fetzek (2021).
24. Greaves (2021a, 2021b).
25. Greaves (2014).
26. Greaves and Gricius (forthcoming).
27. Chater et al. (2020) and Greaves and Lackenbauer (2021).
28. Greaves (2022).
29. Borgerson (2008).
30. Dodds (2010) and Lackenbauer (2010).
31. Lajeunesse and Lackenbauer (2020).
32. Charron (2015), Exner-Pirot (2012), Huebert (2011) and Lackenbauer and Huebert (2014).
33. Lajeunesse (2008).
34. Byers (2009), Byers and Covey (2019), Johnson (2021), Kawasaki (2019) and Østhagen et al. (2018).
35. Parliamentary Information and Research Services (2020).
36. See Justin Trudeau, Prime Minister of Canada. *Mandate Letters* (2019).
37. Barclay et al. (2020).
38. Department of National Defence (2017).
39. Ibid., p. 52.
40. Northern Affairs Canada (2019).
41. Coates and Mitchell (2012), Greaves (2012b) and Gjørv et al. (2014).
42. Greaves (2012a, 2012b) and Smith (2010).
43. Goodman and Baudu (2023).
44. Canadian Security Intelligence Service (2021).
45. United Nations Development Programme (2022).
46. Goodman and Baudu (2023).
47. Gleick (2014), International Committee of the Red Cross (2019), Mitra (2017) and Selby et al. (2017).
48. Hanselpacker (2021).
49. Brown (2008) and The White House (2021).
50. Purdy and Smythe (2010, p. 423).
51. Greaves (2024).
52. Department of National Defence (n.d.).
53. Harvard T.H. Chan School of Public Health (n.d.).
54. Major and Shivji (2019).
55. Berthiaume (2022).
56. Hanselpacker (2021) and Leuprecht and Kasurak (2020).
57. Kikkert and Lackenbauer (2021).
58. Department of National Defence (2017, p. 75).
59. Department of National Defence (2020a).

60. Department of National Defence (2020a, 2020b).
61. Department of National Defence (n.d.).
62. Conflict and Environment Observatory (n.d.).
63. Treasury Board (n.d.).
64. Welsh (2020).
65. Purdy and Smythe (2010, p. 423).
66. Purdy and Smythe (2010) and Greaves (2021a).
67. Greaves (2021b).
68. Pugliese (2022).

References

Anderson, Bruce, and David Coletto. 2017. Public Attitudes on Oil, Pipelines, Climate, and Change. Abacus Data. Available at: https://abacusdata.ca/public-attitudes-on-oil-pipelines-climate-and-change/.

Barclay, Jill, Jayde Lavoie, Carly MacArthur, and Maria Nallim. 2020. Climate Change, Security and Military Preparedness in North America. *North American and Arctic Defence and Security Network*: 6–7. Available at: https://www.naadsn.ca/wp-content/uploads/2020/09/20_September_Climate-Change-Policy-Primer.pdf.

Barnett, Jon. 2001. *The Meaning of Environmental Security: Ecological Politics and Policy in the New Security Era*. London: Zed Books.

Barry, Donald, and Duane Bratt. 2008. Defence Against Help: Explaining Canada-U.S. Security Relations. *American Review of Canadian Studies* 38 (1): 63–89

Berthiaume, Lee. 2022. Disaster Relief a Threat to the Canadian Army's Fighting Edge, Commander Says. *The National Post*. Available at: https://nationalpost.com/news/canada/disaster-relief-threatens-to-hinder-canadian-armys-readiness-for-combat-commander.

Borgerson, Scott. 2008. Arctic Meltdown: The Economic and Security Implications of Global Warming. *Foreign Affairs* 87 (2): 63–77.

Boyd, Brendan. 2019. A Province Under Pressure: Climate Change Policy in Alberta. *Canadian Journal of Political Science* 52 (1): 183–199.

Bradshaw, Corey, et al. 2021. Underestimating the Challenges of Avoiding a Ghastly Future. *Frontiers in Conservation Science* 1: 1–10.

Brown, Lester. 1977. Redefining National Security. *Worldwatch Paper 14*. Washington: Worldwatch Institute.

Brown, Oli. 2008. *Migration and Climate Change*. IOM Migration Research Series No. 31. Geneva: International Organization for Migration.

Byers, Michael. 2009. *Who Owns the Arctic: Understanding Sovereignty Disputes in the North*. Vancouver: Douglas and McIntyre.

Byers, Michael, and Nicole Covey. 2019. Arctic SAR and the Security Dilemma. *International Journal* 74 (1): 499–517.

Bush, Elizabeth, and David S. Lemmen. 2019. *Canada's Changing Climate Report*. Ottawa: Environment and Climate Change Canada.

Buzan, Barry, and Lene Hansen. 2009. *The Evolution of International Security Studies*. Cambridge: Cambridge University Press.

Canadian Security Intelligence Service. 2021. *CSIS Scene Setter: Climate Change Security Factors*. Analytical Brief. CAB 2021-22/02. Ottawa: Canadian Security and Intelligence Service.

Carvin, Stephanie. 2021. *Stand on Guard: Reassessing Threats to Canada's National Security*. Toronto: University of Toronto Press.

Charron, Andrea. 2015. Canada, the Arctic, and NORAD: Status Quo or New Ball Game? *International Journal* 70 (2): 215–231.

Chater, Andrew, Wilfrid Greaves, and Leah Sarson. 2020. Assessing Security Governance in the Arctic. In *Handbook on Arctic Security*, ed. Gunhild Hoogensen Gjørv and Horatio Sam-Aggrey, 43–56. London: Routledge.

Coates, Ken, and Terry Mitchell. 2012. The Rise of the Fourth World. *CIGIOnline*. Available at: https://www.cigionline.org/articles/rise-fourth-world/.

Conflict and Environment Observatory. (n.d.). The Military Emissions Gap. Available at: https://militaryemissions.org/.

Conger, John, and Shiloh Fetzek. 2021. *A Climate Security Plan for Canada: How the Government of Canada Can Combat the Security Risks of Climate Change*. Washington: Center for Climate and Security.

Crutzen, Paul J. 2002. Geology of Mankind. *Nature* 415: 23.

Dalby, Simon. 2002. *Environmental Security*. Minneapolis: University of Minnesota Press.

Dalby, Simon. 2009. *Security and Environmental Change*. Cambridge: Polity.

Dalby, Simon, and Leah Lawrence. 2021. *Climate Change Impacts on Canadian National Security*. Reimagining a Canadian National Security Strategy No. 2. Waterloo: Centre for International Governance Innovation.

Deudney, Daniel H., and Richard A. Matthew. 1999. *Contested Grounds: Security and Conflict in the New Environmental Politics*. Albany: SUNY Press.

Dodds, Klaus. 2010. Flag Planting and Finger Pointing: The Law of the Sea, the Arctic and the Political Geographies of the Outer Continental Shelf. *Political Geography* 29 (2): 63–73.

Exner-Pirot, Heather. 2012. Defence Diplomacy in the Arctic: The Search and Rescue Agreement as a Confidence Builder. *Canadian Foreign Policy Journal* 18 (2): 195–207.

Fewster, Richard, et al. 2022. Imminent Loss of Climate Space for Permafrost Peatlands in Europe and Western Siberia. *Nature Climate Change* 12: 373–379.

Floyd, Rita, and Richard A. Matthew. 2013. *Environmental Security: Approaches and Issues*. New York: Routledge.

Gjørv, Hoogensen, Dawn Bazely Gunhild, Marina Goloviznina, and Andrew Tanentzap. 2014. *Environmental and Human Security in the Arctic*. New York: Routledge.

Gleick, Peter H. 2014. Water, Drought, Climate Change, and Conflict in Syria. *Weather, Climate, and Society* 6 (3): 331–340.

Goodman, Sherri, and Pauline Baudu. 2023. *Climate Change as a 'Threat Multiplier': History, Uses and Future of the Concept*. Briefer No. 38. Washington: Center for Climate and Security. Available at: https://climateandsecurity.org/2023/01/briefer-climate-change-as-a-threat-multiplier-history-uses-and-future-of-the-concept/#:~:text=The%20term%20was%20denied%20in,to%20contribute%20to%20security%20risks.

Government of Canada, Department of National Defence. 2017. Strong, Secure, Engaged: Canada's Defence Policy. Available at https://www.canada.ca/en/department-national-defence/corporate/reports-publications/canada-defence-policy.htm.

Government of Canada, Department of National Defence. 2020a. *Defence Energy and Environment Strategy 2020–2023*. Ottawa: Government of Canada. Available at: https://www.canada.ca/en/department-national-defence/corporate/reports-publications/dees.html.

Government of Canada, Department of National Defence. 2020b. Strong, Secure, Engaged: Moving to Sustainable Defence Operations. Available at: https://www.canada.ca/en/department-national-defence/maple-leaf/defence/2020/02/strong-secure-engaged-moving-to-sustainable-defence-operations.html.

Government of Canada, Department of National Defence. (n.d.). *Defence Energy and Environment Strategy (DEES) 2021–2022 Results Report*. Ottawa: Department of National Defence. Available at: https://www.canada.ca/en/department-national-defence/corporate/reports-publications/dees/dees-2021-2022-results-report.html.

Government of Canada, Department of National Defence. (n.d.). *Operation LENTUS*. Ottawa: Government of Canada. Available at: https://www.canada.ca/en/department-national-defence/services/operations/military-operations/current-operations/operation-lentus.html.

Government of Canada, Treasury Board. (n.d.). *Government of Canada's Greenhouse Gas Emissions Inventory*. Ottawa: Government of Canada. Available at: https://www.canada.ca/en/treasury-board-secretariat/services/innovation/greening-government/government-canada-greenhouse-gas-emissions-inventory.html.

Greaves, Wilfrid. 2012a. For Whom, From What? Canada's Arctic Policy and the Narrowing of Human Security. *International Journal* 67 (1): 219–240.

Greaves, Wilfrid. 2012b. Insecurities of Non-dominance: Re-Theorizing Human Security and Environmental Change in Developed States. In *Natural Resources and Social Conflict: Towards Critical Environmental Security*, ed. Matthew A. Schnurr and Larry A. Swatuk, 63–82. New York: Palgrave.

Greaves, Wilfrid. 2014. Naturally Insecure: Critical Environmental Security and Critical Security Studies in Canada. *Critical Studies on Security* 1: 81–104.

Greaves, Wilfrid. 2020. Democracy, Donald Trump, and the Canada-U.S. Security Community. *Canadian Journal of Political Science* 53 (4): 800–820.

Greaves, Wilfrid. 2021a. Climate Change and Security in Canada. *International Journal* 76 (2): 183–203.

Greaves, Wilfrid. 2021b. What Would It Mean to Treat Climate Change Like a Security Threat? CIGIOnline. Waterloo: Centre for International Governance Innovation. https://www.cigionline.org/articles/what-would-it-mean-to-treat-climate-as-a-security-risk/.

Greaves, Wilfrid. 2022. The New Arctic Geopolitics. *RUSI Commentary*. Royal United Services Institute. Available at: https://rusi.org/explore-our-research/publications/commentary/new-arctic-geopolitics.

Greaves, Wilfrid. 2024. Human Security, Climate Change, and the Role of the Canadian Armed Forces: British Columbia, 2021. *Canadian Military Journal*. Special Issue on "Climate Change and Security."

Greaves Wilfrid, and Gabriella Gricius. (Forthcoming). Climate Change, Environmental Diplomacy, and Arctic Security. *Canadian Foreign Policy Journal*. Special Issue on "Situating the Arctic in Canadian Foreign Policy Analysis".

Greaves, Wilfrid, and P. Whitney Lackenbauer. 2021. *Breaking Through: Understanding Sovereignty and Security in the Circumpolar Arctic*. Toronto: University of Toronto Press.

Hanselpacker, Gabriel J. 2021. Climate Change and the Canadian Armed Forces. Thesis, Master of Defence Studies, Canadian Forces College.

Harrington, Cameron, and Clifford Shearing. 2017. *Security in the Anthropocene: Reflections on Safety and Care*. New York: Columbia University Press.

Harvard T.H. Chan School of Public Health. (n.d) Coronavirus and Climate Change. Available at: https://www.hsph.harvard.edu/c-change/subtopics/coronavirus-and-climate-change/.

Homer-Dixon, Thomas. 1991. On the Threshold: Environmental Changes as Causes of Acute Conflict. *International Security* 16 (2): 76–116.

Homer-Dixon, Thomas. 1994. Environmental Scarcities and Violent Conflict: Evidence from Cases. *International Security* 19 (1): 5–40.

Homer-Dixon, Thomas. 1999. *Environment, Scarcity, and Violence*. Princeton: Princeton University Press.

Homer-Dixon, Thomas, and Jessica Blitt. 1998. *Ecoviolence: Links Among Environment, Population, and Security*. Boston: Rowman & Littlefield.

Huebert, Rob. 2011. Submarines, Oil Tankers, and Icebreakers: Trying to Understand Canadian Arctic Sovereignty and Security. *International Journal* 66 (4): 809–824.

Intergovernmental Panel on Climate Change. 2022. Summary for Policymakers. Contribution of Working Group II to the Sixth Assessment Report of the Intergovernmental Panel on Climate Change, ed. H.-O. Pörtner, D.C. Roberts, M. Tignor, E.S. Poloczanska, K. Mintenbeck, A. Alegría, M. Craig, S. Langsdorf, S. Löschke, V. Möller, A. Okem, B. Rama. Cambridge: Cambridge University Press.

International Committee of the Red Cross. 2019. Mali-Niger: Climate Change and Conflict Make an Explosive Mix in the Sahel. *International Committee of the Red Cross*. Available at: https://www.icrc.org/en/document/mali-niger-climate-change-and-conflict-make-explosive-mix-sahel.

Johnson, Benjamin T. 2021. Sensing the Arctic: Situational Awareness and the Future of Northern Security. *International Journal* 76 (3): 404–426.

Kawasaki, Tsuyoshi. 2019. Canada as a Peninsula State: Conceptualizing the Emerging Geopolitical Landscape in the 21st Century. *International Journal* 74 (3): 345–362.

Keeble, Edna. 2005. Defining Canadian Security: Continuities and Discontinuities. *American Review of Canadian Studies* 35 (1): 1–23.

Kikkert Peter. 2021. Creating a Non-military Disaster Workforce Must be Part of Canada's Climate Change Response. *North American and Arctic Defence and Security Network Policy Brief*. Available at: https://www.naadsn.ca/wp-content/uploads/2021/12/21-dec-Kikkert-Disaster-Workforce-Policy-Brief.pdf.

Kikkert, Peter, and P. Whitney Lackenbauer. 2021. The Canadian Rangers: Strengthening Community Disaster Resilience in Canada's Remote and Isolated Communities. *The Northern Review* 51: 1–33.

Krause, Keith, and Michael C. Williams. 1996. Broadening the Agenda of Security Studies: Politics and Methods. *Mershon International Studies Review* 40 (2): 229–254.

Justin Trudeau, Prime Minister of Canada. 2019. *Mandate Letters*. Available at: https://pm.gc.ca/en/mandate-letters.

Lackenbauer, P. Whitney. 2010. Mirror Images? Canada, Russia, and the Circumpolar World. *International Journal* 65 (4): 879–897.

Lackenbauer, P. Whitney., and Rob Huebert. 2014. Premier Partners: Canada, the United States and Arctic Security. *Canadian Foreign Policy Journal* 20 (3): 320–333.

Lagassé, Philippe. 2010. Nils Ørvik's 'Defence Against Help': The Descriptive Appeal of a Prescriptive Strategy. *International Journal* 65 (2): 463–474.

Lajeunesse, Adam. 2008. The Northwest Passage in Canadian Policy: An Approach for the 21st Century. *International Journal* 63 (4): 1037–1052.

Lajeunesse, Adam, and P. Whitney Lackenbauer. 2020. Defence Policy in the Canadian Arctic: From Jean Chrétien to Justin Trudeau. In *Canadian Defence Policy in Theory and Practice*, ed. Thomas Juneau, Philippe Lagassé, and Srdjan Vucetic, 365–382. London: Palgrave Macmillan.

Lennox, Patrick. 2007. From Golden Straightjacket to Kevlar Vest: Canada's Transformation to a Security State. *Canadian Journal of Political Science* 40 (4): 1017–1038.

Lenton, Timothy M. 2012. Arctic Climate Tipping Points. *Ambio* 41 (1): 10–22.

Lenton, Timothy M., et al. 2008. Tipping Elements in the Earth's Climate System. *Proceedings of the National Academy of Sciences* 105 (6): 1786–1793.

Leuprecht, Christian, and Peter Kasurak. 2020. The Canadian Armed Forces and Humanitarian Assistance and Disaster Relief: Defining a Role. CIGI Online. Available at: https://www.cigionline.org/articles/canadian-armed-forces-and-humanitarian-assistance-and-disaster-relief-defining-role/.

Major, Darren, and Salimah Shivji. 2019. Canada's Military Feeling the Strain Responding to Climate Change. CBC News. Available at: https://www.cbc.ca/news/politics/canada-s-military-adopting-climate-change-1.5186337.

Mathews, Jessica Tuchman. 1989. Redefining Security. *Foreign Affairs* 68 (2): 162–177.

McBean, Gordan A., Idowu Ajibade, Dianne Cunningham, Burt Dowsett, Melissa Harris, Rob Lannigan, Christopher Popovich, Elizabeth Riddell-Dixon, Caroline Rodgers, and Slobodan P. Simonovic. 2021. *The Security of Canada and Canadians: Implications of Climate Change*. London: The University of Western Ontario.

Mitra, Shreya. 2017. Mali's Fertile Grounds for Conflict: Climate Change and Resource Stress. *Planetary Security Initiative*. Available at: https://www.clingendael.org/sites/default/files/2017-12/PB_Malis_Fertile_Grounds_for_Conflict.pdf.

Northern Affairs Canada. 2019. Canada's Arctic and Northern Policy Framework. Available at: https://www.rcaanc-cirnac.gc.ca/eng/1560523306861/1560523330587.

Nossal, Kim Richard. 2004. Defending the 'Realm': Canadian Strategic Culture Revisited. *International Journal* 59 (3): 503–520.

Østhagen, Andreas, Gregory Levi Sharp, and Paal Sigurd Hilde. 2018. At Opposite Poles: Canada's and Norway's Approaches to Security in the Arctic. *The Polar Journal* 8 (1): 163–181.

Parliamentary Information and Research Services. 2020. *Climate Change: Its Impact and Policy Implications*. Ottawa: Library of Parliament. Available at: https://lop.parl.ca/staticfiles/PublicWebsite/Home/ResearchPublications/BackgroundPapers/PDF/2019-46-e.pdf.

Potsdam Institute for Climate Impact Research and Climate Analytics. 2013. *Turn Down the Heat: Climate Extremes, Regional Impacts, and the Case for Resilience*. A Report for the World Bank. Washington: World Bank.

Preston, Jen. 2017. Racial Extractivism and White Settler Colonialism: An Examination of the Canadian Tar Sands Mega-Projects. *Cultural Studies* 31 (2–3): 353–375.

Pugliese, David. 2022. Canadian Forces Officers Applaud Speech Slamming Canada's Climate Change Policies, Cancel Culture, Weak Leaders. *Ottawa Citizen*. Available at: https://ottawacitizen.com/news/national/defence-watch/speech-slamming-canadas-climate-change-policies-cancel-culture-and-weak-leaders-applauded-by-canadian-forces-officers.

Purdy, Margaret, and Leanne Smythe. 2010. From Obscurity to Action: Why Canada Must Tackle the Security Dimensions of Climate Change. *International Journal* 65 (2): 411–420.

Renner, Michael. 1989. *National Security: The Economic and Environmental Dimensions*. Worldwatch Paper 89. Washington: Worldwatch Institute.

Rockström, Johan, et al. 2009. A Safe Operating Space for Humanity. *Nature* 461 (7263): 472–475.

Rothschild, Emma. 1995. What Is Security? *Daedalus* 124 (3): 53–98.

Selby, Jan, Omar Dahi, Christiane Fröhlich, and Mike Hulme. 2017. Climate Change and the Syrian Civil War Revisited. *Political Geography* 60: 232–244.

Smith, Steve. 2005. The Contested Concept of Security. In *Critical Security Studies and World Politics*, ed. Ken Booth, 27–62. Boulder: Lynn Rienner.

Smith, Heather A. 2010. Choosing Not to See: Canada, Climate Change, and the Arctic. *International Journal* 65 (4): 931–942.

The White House. 2021. *Report on the Impact of Climate Change on Migration*. Washington: The White House.

Ullman, Richard H. 1983. Redefining Security. *International Security* 8 (1): 129–153.

United Nations. (n.d.). Climate Action. Available at: https://www.un.org/en/climatechange/un-secretary-general-speaks-state-planet.

United Nations Development Programme. 2022. *New Threats to Human Security in the Anthropocene*. New York: United Nations Development Report.

Walt, Stephen M. 1991. The Renaissance of Security Studies. *International Studies Quarterly* 35 (2): 211–239.

Welsh, Kyle. 2020. *A Win-Win Strategy for the Government of Canada: A Plan for the RCAF to Reduce Greenhouse Gas Emissions While Remaining Operationally Effective*. JCPS 46 Solo Flight. Toronto: Canadian Forces College.

Winfield, Mark, Vanessa Scanga, and Peter McKenna. 2022. International Climate Change Policy in the Harper Era. In *Harper's World: The Politicization of Canadian Foreign Policy, 2006–2015*, ed. Peter McKenna, 99–123. Toronto: University of Toronto Press.

Wolfers, Arnold. 1952. 'National Security' as an Ambiguous Symbol. *Political Science Quarterly* 67 (4): 481–502.

NORAD Modernization: Past, Present and Future

Andrea Charron and James Fergusson

On 13 February 2017, a bilateral commitment to modernize the North American Aerospace Defence Command (NORAD) was announced in a joint statement following the first meeting of American President Donald Trump and Canadian Prime Minister Justin Trudeau.[1] Several months later, NORAD modernization was identified as a priority in Canada's 2017 defence policy, *Strong, Secure and Engaged*. Following the 2019 Federal Election, the Prime Minister's mandate letter to the Minister of National Defence (MND), Harjit Sajjan, reiterated this commitment.[2]

Parts of this paper were published by Macdonald-Laurier Institute as James Fergusson, "North American Defence Modernization in an Uncertain Age" (October 2022). The authors are grateful for permission to use parts of that commentary. See Fergusson (2022).

A. Charron (✉) · J. Fergusson
Department of Political Studies, University of Manitoba, Winnipeg, MB, Canada
e-mail: Andrea.Charron@umanitoba.ca

J. Fergusson
e-mail: James.Fergusson@umanitoba.ca

© The Author(s), under exclusive license to Springer Nature Switzerland AG 2023
T. Juneau and P. Lagassé (eds.), *Canadian Defence Policy in Theory and Practice, Volume 2*, Canada and International Affairs,
https://doi.org/10.1007/978-3-031-37542-2_5

Another two years later, in the joint statement following the first (virtual) meeting between President Joseph Biden and Prime Minister Trudeau, continental defence cooperation and NORAD modernization were again emphasized.[3]

Throughout this period, few if any details were provided regarding the scope and breadth of modernization, nor did the government commit any funds.[4] This began to change in 2021. The Federal Government committed $252 million in the 2021 budget to "lay the groundwork for NORAD's future[…] and sustain existing continental and Arctic defence capabilities."[5] On 14 August 2021, a joint statement on NORAD modernization by MND Sajjan and the United States (US) Secretary of Defense (SecDef) Lloyd James Austin III was released.[6] Specifically, the statement identified four broad areas of modernization: situational awareness; modernized command and control (C^2); capabilities to deter and, if necessary, defeat evolving aerospace threats to North America, and research and development.

In the 2022 Canadian federal budget, $8 billion in new funding over five years was added to the defence budget, although the amount committed to NORAD modernization was unspecified.[7] On 22 June 2022, MND Anand announced $4.9 billion over six years, and $40 billion over twenty years for modernization with only some details.[8] A month later on July 21st, the Department of National Defence (DND) provided more details. Relative to the August 2021 joint statement/agreement, the Department inserted a fifth area partially related to modernization—ensuring the ability of the Canadian Armed Forces (CAF) to "launch and sustain a strong military presence across the country, including in Canada's North, through investments in new infrastructure and support capabilities"—and broke down the $40 billion investment by each area.[9] On 24 March 2023, when President Biden addressed Parliament, Canada announced an accelerated time frame for some of the NORAD projects focusing especially on domain awareness. An increase in funding to support the acceleration, however, was not announced.[10]

Overall, NORAD modernization is just beginning, and with it are a much broader and deeper set of issues concerning the NORAD Agreement, NORAD's existing missions and the future of continental and North American defence cooperation, which have largely been ignored to date. In order to place the current, official parameters of NORAD modernization relative to these issues in order, it is important to appreciate NORAD's past and the new strategic, technological and geopolitical environment that emerged roughly in 2014. This, in turn, provides the foundation for examining the current state or parameters of NORAD modernization. Finally, they provide the basis for identifying and analysing the broader and deeper set of issues that lurk beneath the surface, and their implications for the future of North American defence and continued cooperation.

In other words, the current framework of NORAD modernization, as laid out in the aforementioned documents by the Canadian government, remains firmly embedded in the past, even though the international political, strategic and technological threat environments have been transformed radically. Responding to this new environment will require, if not dictate, a new and expanded NORAD as the centrepiece of Canada-US defence cooperation not only in terms of North America, but also globally. This, in turn, carries with it major political implications for future Canadian defence policies and budgets.

NORAD Modernization and the New Threat Environment

North American continental defence has largely been a secondary, if not tertiary, priority for both Canada and the United States, exhibiting long periods of relative neglect interspersed by brief flurries of investment, usually prompted by technological developments and equipment life cycles. Instead, both governments, or more accurately defence departments, have long prioritized overseas commitments as the key to the defence of North America. This has been reinforced, at least since the early 1960s to the end of the Cold War, by the reliance upon American strategic nuclear deterrence to protect North America. Any potential attack against North America was assumed to be a strategic nuclear one, and, until just recently, there was no means to defend against it. Instead, this attack was deterred by the American threat of strategic nuclear retaliation under the condition of Mutual Assured Destruction (MAD).

In this context, NORAD played a key role as a function of its ballistic missile early warning mission, acquired in the 1960s. Accessing information from the US Ballistic Missile Early Warning System (BMEWS), NORAD's mission was to assess whether North America was under attack, and if so, characterize the nature of the attack and inform the National Command Authorities (NCA)—a mission labelled Integrated

Tactical Warning/Attack Assessment (ITW/AA). Although both countries' NCA would be notified, the key decision-maker was the US President, with the authority to order a retaliatory strike. In effect, the American strategic nuclear retaliatory deterrent made North America a sanctuary and significantly reduced capability and investment requirements.

Certainly, the Soviet Union's long-range bomber threat had not disappeared during this period, although it was relatively marginal per se, as evident in the dramatic reduction in air defence assets assigned to NORAD's air control mission in the 1960s and 70s.[11] Even so, three factors would lead to modernization in the 1980s. First, the radar lines established in the 1950s were approaching obsolescence and the end of their life cycle. Second, the air-breathing threat environment took a technological leap forward with the development and deployment of air launched cruise missiles (ALCMs). Finally, the United States formally adopted the countervailing strategy in 1980, which would subsequently be termed the "warfighting" strategy.[12] Combined, they became the fundamental defence rationale for the modernization of NORAD's air early warning system with the deployment of the North Warning System (NWS), not fully operational until 1993. The end of the Cold War eliminated the main threat (the USSR), and with the modernized NWS, a new era of continental defence neglect emerged, only slightly altered in the wake of 9/11 with the integration of internal Canadian and US civil radar feeds into NORAD to have a more "complete" North American operational picture.[13]

These patterns of the past are now recurring, but the transformative implications for NORAD and continental defence are much greater than in the past. As early as 2011, defence officials recognized that the NWS would reach the end of its serviceable life around 2025. Furthermore, its modernization would require that its radar reach be extended farther north to match the full extent of Canada's Arctic archipelago and the "realignment" of Canada's Air Defence Identification Zone (CADIZ) in 2018 to match Canadian territory.[14] At roughly the same time, the threat environment began to change significantly, rendering the NWS functionally obsolete and making what would have been a relatively straightforward, simple modernization process much more technically complicated, costly and time sensitive.

Around 2011, intelligence reported that Russia had developed a new generation of very long-range air- and sea-launched cruise missiles. Such missiles could be deployed beyond the reach of NWS radars, which had been optimized to identify, track and vector fighters to intercept the launch platforms—bombers or "archers" in NORAD parlance—before they reached their launch points.[15] This new technological threat environment was magnified with the subsequent Russian development of hypersonic weapons around 2017.[16] Alongside these new threats, Russia is developing nuclear powered cruise missiles, and, partially as a function of the collapse of the Intermediate Nuclear Forces (INF) Treaty in 2019, may develop long-range ground-launched cruise missiles.

Politically, relations with Russia had already begun to deteriorate following the Russian cyber attack on Estonia in 2007 and its war with Georgia in 2008. Relations worsened with direct Russian military involvement in the Syrian Civil War and its subsequent annexation of Crimea and direct military support to the separatist movements in Eastern Ukraine following the 2014 Ukrainian Maidan Revolution. At the same time, China had undertaken provocative actions in East Asia, especially around the South China Sea, and had significantly modernized and expanded its military capabilities.

The role of nuclear weapons in American strategic thinking has also changed significantly. In successive US Nuclear Posture Review documents, the need to maintain strategic nuclear forces was reiterated, but their purpose was ill-defined because there was no one to deter per se. The Soviet Union had collapsed, and its successor, Russia was crippled by economic, political and social re-construction. In addition, the US and Russian strategic nuclear arsenals began to decline significantly as a function of the Strategic Arms Reduction Treaties (START) but Russia abandoned the New START in 2023— the last remaining nuclear weapons treaty between the United States and Russia. It would seem the importance of nuclear weapons has taken a back seat to American conventional military capabilities. Nuclear weapons and strategic nuclear deterrence is now conceptualized as the weapon of last resort in contrast to the Cold War when it was the weapon of first resort.[17] In line with this thinking, the dominant continental deterrence and defence narrative conceives of new generations of Russian and Chinese non-ballistic missile capabilities as a conventional threat against North America.[18] Their objective is to alter the US', and to a lesser degree Canadian decision-making calculations by holding critical North American economic infrastructure hostage, by threatening to attack embarkation points in North America to deter overseas intervention, and, if deterrence fails, dramatically challenge the ability of the United States and Canada to support and move forces overseas. In basic terms, North America is vulnerable and no longer a sanctuary from conventional war. Unless vulnerability is eliminated, Russia and China will be emboldened to act in their respective regions and discount the US-led global deterrent posture.

North America lacks the detection and defeat capabilities to deal with this new technological, political and strategic threat environment and ensure a credible deterrence by denial posture vital to continental defence. Consequentially, continental defence modernization, largely, if not exclusively for Canada conceptualized as NORAD modernization, has emerged as a priority for both Canada and the United States.[19]

The Current State and Parameters of NORAD Modernization

NORAD modernization is just beginning even though the requirements to modernize date back roughly a decade, given the approaching end of the NWS' life cycle and the new threat environment. The delay may be attributed to technical and political considerations. Technically, to confront the new threat environment, and thus ensure an effective North American deterrent posture, a more complicated and integrated multi-domain warning system is required—one that stands in contrast to the NWS, which is single domain, land-based radar systems that stretch across the Canadian Arctic and down the coast of Labrador. Not only do the land-based radars need to be more powerful and capable of reaching far over-the-horizon to track cruise and hypersonic missiles in flight, but it also needs to be augmented by space (a future unspecified Canadian investment), air and potentially maritime-based capabilities, and linked into NORAD command, control and communications.[20]

The new system requires the development of a new architecture and the development and acquisition of new technologies, and these take a significant amount of time prior to making investment decisions. Relatedly, these developments cannot be taken in isolation of American decisions and plans, especially as it has commitments to NORAD modernization and is the primary source for new technologies. Negotiating and reaching an agreement requires patience.

Politically, several interrelated considerations have been at play since 2011. A consensus must emerge on the threats and their priorities, and this has long been difficult in Canada and the United States because political and military attention has generally focused on overseas commitments and capability requirements "over there."[21] North America, NORAD and the Arctic component in particular are politically sensitive domestic issues because of longstanding Canadian sovereignty concerns relative to the United States. As such, North American defence cooperation is always liable to the general state of relations between Canada and the United States, and one of the reasons why Ottawa has preferred NORAD to operate beneath the political radar in Canada.[22]

Canadian concerns about the Trump presidency and focus on NAFTA negotiations arguably made progress in the NORAD modernization file politically risky and, as such, one might interpret the 2017 commitment *sans details* and money as a political trial balloon. The election of President Biden in 2020, however, changed the political climate. In addition, the Russian invasion of Ukraine eliminated any potential domestic, political opposition to NORAD modernization which one might have expected with charges of "militarizing" the Arctic and "kowtowing" to the Americans—the perennial Canadian arguments cited to brake spending on military capabilities.

Regardless of the delay, the foundation for NORAD modernization now exists, as laid out in the August 2021 Joint Statement on NORAD Modernization (Department of Defense, 2021). The requirement to mount a credible deterrence by denial posture for continental defence requires the acquisition of new detection and defeat capabilities to deter not only threats to North America, but also for global deterrence requirements. These, in turn, are broken down in the Canadian case into five areas for investment.[23] The first is situational awareness which requires the ability to detect and track these new threats from launch through flight. NWS modernization or renewal is only one component and requires a new generation of over-the-horizon radars capable of cruise and, if possible, hypersonic vehicle detection (Pugliese 2022). The balloon incidents in February 2023[24] are also a reminder that NORAD must be able to detect slower moving air objects as well. Two over-the-horizon ground-based radar lines will be established—an "Arctic" line near the Canada-US southern border and a polar line across the Canadian high Arctic.[25] The latter will not be operational for many years, but the former's timeline has been accelerated for initial operation in 2028. Because of the complicated nature of the threat environment, these ground-based radars will also need to be supplemented by air, maritime and space-based detection capabilities—the latter of which has been identified without any specific details as to type. In addition, these detection capabilities need to be extended around the continent to provide 360° all-domain coverage of North America, although Canada's commitment is focused on the northern approaches especially from ten o'clock to two o'clock.

The second priority is to modernize command, control and communication systems, reflecting the need to integrate and exploit the situational awareness that the "system-of-systems" will (ideally) bring. To ensure detection, tracking, target discrimination, the cueing of interception capabilities, and provision of battle damage assessment, many complicated systems and cloud-based data will need to be gathered, distributed, assessed and acted on. This requires new advanced, redundant communication systems to avoid a single point of failure, and the technology to process and analyse the large volume of data generated by the integrated sensor systems. The physical architecture needed to transport this data means that current command and control centres will need upgrading and cyber 'hardening' as well. The 2021 NORAD and USNORTHCOM strategy captures this second priority as a linear strategy with three interlinked requirements: all-domain awareness which provides information dominance and decision-superiority championed by NORAD Commander General VanHerck (2021–2023).

The third priority is the interception or defeat side of the NORAD modernization equation with concentration on air weapons systems. For some time now, and reflecting the Cold War past, the preferred interceptor solution to the non-ballistic missile threat had been to target the launch platforms or "archers" (i.e. the ubiquitous Bear bomber). However, this has become problematic in two ways. First, preventing a launch requires potentially targeting platforms far from North American territory in the Arctic and thus requires new in-flight re-fuelling capabilities[26] and the modernization of northern forward operating locations (FOLs) enabling the RCAF to be in range of potential launch platforms. Of course, a more flexible solution is forward deployed naval anti-submarine assets, but decisions about replacing submarines in Canada have been slow and politically divisive. For now, Canada has only committed to the acquisition of new generation of short, medium and long-range air-to-air missiles in addition to the desperately needed refuelling capabilities and modernization/reanimation of Arctic-based-FOLs. Even with extended range capabilities, however, it is questionable whether intercepting the platforms is truly feasible, whether there are sufficient interceptors to undertake this task, and, as no defence is perfect, confront the probability of having to intercept cruise missiles and hypersonics in flight. In other words, NORAD is now in the missile defence or "arrows'" world.

The fourth area is sustaining a strong military presence across the country, including in Canada's North, through investments in new infrastructure and support capabilities especially air-to-air refuellers. There are also hints that any new infrastructure, especially in the Arctic, will be multi-purpose to provide benefits local residents and other government departments.

The fifth priority, and particular to Canada, is to "future proof" defence capabilities especially through investment in research, development and innovation to acquire the technologies vital to modernize and keep pace with future developments. In other words, the days of 'one and done' legacy projects (such as updating the Distant Early Warning line to the NWS) are over. Constant renewals and improvements (presumably with AI and quantum computing) will ensure capabilities keep pace with changing technology.

Although both the National Defence Fact Sheet and Joint Statement on NORAD Modernization are short on details, especially concerning timelines for implementation and specific US financial and other contributions, it can be inferred from the Canadian funding commitment that this will be a twenty-year process, in which capabilities will emerge in a sequential or iterative manner.[27] Most pressing is arguably the Arctic over-the-horizon radar (OTHR) system (to provide radar coverage into the Arctic and east coast). The Polar version faces numerous technological and logistical challenges. The first is interference from the effect of the aurora borealis.[28] There are also questions about the energy sources for the radars (will they be 'green'?), location of the radars and their transmission and receiver sites, opportunities for employment and training for northerners, opportunities to make the radars multi-purpose to collect and disseminate information to other government departments and the potential interference with other existing government radar and communication systems. Both OTHR systems require the deployment of new command, control and communication capabilities to ensure its effectiveness—all of which will take time to build, test, implement and render operational. North America and Canada, therefore, will remain vulnerable for some time to come.

In addition, the modernization plans face other time barriers. Building new radar lines, or any other NORAD-related Arctic infrastructure, is no easy task, with a short construction season, and limited maritime transportation capacity and large distances to travel.[29] Alongside this reality, six years, relative to the $4.9 billion committed in June 2022, is a very short time in the historically lengthy Canadian procurement process with an average closer to fifteen years. Assuming that the internal specification of requirements process has been completed for the unspecified first six-year stage, requests for proposals or bids must be issued, companies (assuming Canadian companies have such expertise) need to construct their bids taking into account buy Canadian provisions in terms of industrial and technological benefits, as well as the government's commitment to significant Indigenous participation. Next, the bids must be evaluated, contracts issued and finally the acquisition and deployment undertaken.[30] Where this all stands today is unknown publicly and the accelerated timeline for some of the projects are aspirational at best.

In other words, the likelihood that DND can spend $4.9 billion over six years appears low. Certainly, the government can streamline the process by invoking national security and undertaking non-competitive, off-the-shelf buys. However, this is highly unlikely given the Trudeau government's decision to pursue a competition for the CF-18 replacement project (the F35 was ultimately chosen), and the defence minister's statement in Trenton that assured Canadians that "[modernization] will create tremendous opportunities for Canadian industry, and [...] will ensure that Indigenous owned-businesses benefit from these investments, throughout the supply chain".[31]

If DND is unable to spend $4.9 billion over six years, what then happens to the unspent portion? In the past, National Defence has returned unspent money to the central agencies, never to be seen again. There is no National Defence savings account. Of course, conceived as simply part of the $40 billion twenty-year NORAD funding commitment, the unspent amount may not be affected, but this remains to be seen.

What is more, twenty years is a very long time in the political, economic and technological world. While Presidents Trump and Biden and Prime Minister Trudeau have committed to the current NORAD modernization plans, much can transpire between now and 2042. At least five federal elections will occur, and the degree to which future governments remain committed to defence of the continent (the perennial forgotten, nondiscretionary requirement) is unpredictable. Nor is the current international environment set in stone. No one can predict the state of western relations with Russia as the future unfolds, not to mention relations with China. No one can predict whether the apparent political and public consensus on defence and NORAD modernization will hold. No one can realistically predict the state of the economy over the next year or so, never mind in twenty years. National Defence will not be immune from government fiscal retrenchment or demands to re-direct funds during an economic downturn to other more politically salient economic and social pressures.

As well, and if history is our guide, the actual final costs of NORAD modernization are likely to exceed significantly $40 billion, especially given the unpredictable costs of acquiring new advanced technologies for the NORAD mission suite as they emerge over the next twenty years. The Royal Canadian Navy's future surface combatant ship strategy is a case in point, with numerous cost overruns and time extensions. And there are no guarantees that the US Department of Defense will stay the course. They may find other partners and/or work arounds (including more space-based systems that circumscribe Canadian involvement), especially if Canadian progress is considered too slow. Finally, the biggest question for NORAD modernization is what can be accomplished in the context of NORAD versus continental defence writ large without reopening the binational NORAD agreement?

Determining what plans are limited to a NORAD-only context and what plans and priorities extend to both wider continental defence modernization needs as well as Canadian-specific needs are hard to separate. Of note here is the aforementioned unique Canadian fifth area of investment, which can be interpreted as Canadian homeland defence, not NORAD modernization relative to the 2021 Joint Statement on NORAD Modernization. Importantly, NORAD is a supported command as a function of Canadian and American commitments of resources to it. In this sense, future Canadian-based sensors are not NORAD-only assets. If in Canadian territory, they will be maintained and owned by Canada, with the hope they also serve other civilian functions. Today at least in the Canadian case, Canada's funding commitments all appear under the umbrella of NORAD modernization, and what portion is truly NORAD is an open question. Thus, for example, in a recent presentation, DND's Chief Financial Officer identified $87 billion as the total twenty-year funding cash commitment, of which $50 billion is for infrastructure without specifying or breaking down the total (CGAI 2022).

NORAD modernization is also firmly set within the existing parameters of the NORAD Agreement; its terms of reference and existing mission suites of aerospace warning, aerospace (air) control and maritime warning dating back to the 2006 Renewal Agreement in which the agreement was signed in perpetuity and the maritime warning mission was added. It appears that neither Canada nor the United States have an interest or desire to re-open the Agreement, even though the threat environment has transformed since 2006. Instead, the hope is that the technologically-driven modernization plans will not necessitate a change to the 2006 terms. However, technology is never politically and operationally neutral and it is likely that the modernization plans will have more significant implications for NORAD and the future of CANUS North American defence cooperation than currently assumed.

Structural and Political Implications of NORAD Modernization

Although modernization is currently technically driven within the existing NORAD Agreement and missions, it has several significant implications for the future of continental defence cooperation and for NORAD. The first concerns the existing command and control (C^2) structure, which, in turn, entails two basic components. The current C^2 structure, dating back to its origins and consisting of three regional command centres (Alaska, Canada and US Continental Headquarters) is already under consideration. Although the concept of a Combined Forces Air Component Commander (CFACC), experimented in NORAD exercises after 2015, appears to have been shelved, it is clear that a new command and control structure and process are in the offing. Its implications for the regional commands, and thus Canada, remain to be seen.

Closely related, the necessity to modernize C^2 also follows from the integrated multi or pan domain nature of the new surveillance system even though Canada's contribution is dominated by the ground replacement component, now termed the Northern Approaches Surveillance System (NASS). This integration and modernized C^2, in turn, raises questions about the intercept or defeat side of continental deterrence by denial, in which NORAD is limited to the air side of the equation. In other words, multi-domain surveillance integration suggests the need for multi-domain interception or defeat integration to ensure unity of command and effort and eliminate vulnerable domain seams.[32] This is driven by US multi-domain integration developments, indicative in the previous NORAD Commander's emphasis on obtaining Joint All Domain Command and Control (JADC^2). Although the current Commander, US General Glen VanHerck, has dropped it from the NORAD lexicon, it remains in play in the United States military generally and is implicitly embedded in his objective to ensure that NORAD has all-domain awareness, information dominance and decision superiority for deterrence, defence and warfighting.[33] Thus, an expanded integrated multi-domain passive and active mission suite appears as a logical by-product in response to the new threat environment and the proposed technological solutions.

More specifically, naval and air defence assets have historically been transferred under NORAD command as necessary.[34] However, given the importance of forward deployed naval assets to deal with the ocean approaches and the compressed decision-making timeline with modern technology, this appears as a non-optimal solution. Adding a maritime control mission in the context of NORAD's existing maritime warning mission (added in 2006) is an obvious solution. This also raises (in the somewhat distant future) the issue of space capabilities in the equation.

Expanding NORAD's mission suite as a logical solution also extends into considerations of the place of Greenland and to a lesser degree Iceland in the defence of North America. Historically, both have resided within NATO/US European Command's area of operations and neither has ever been considered in Canadian thinking as part of North American defence. Today, however, given potential long-range cruise (air or sea-launched) and hypersonic missile launch points and flight paths down the east coast of Greenland, surveillance and interception coverage needs to be extended and integrated into NORAD. What is more, the US base in Thule Greenland (renamed Pituffik Space Base) and the Danish Joint Arctic Command in Nuuk are essential for both Canada and the United States to refuel and resupply North American Arctic operations. Alternatively, leaving this to bilateral agreements between the United States and Greenland/Denmark is not necessarily an optimal solution for Canada (and this may also extend to Iceland).[35]

The other alternative is the NORAD-NATO status quo where NORAD continues to focus solely on North America and NATO's interests are directed to Europe relative to the sea lines of communication and the North Atlantic as its backdoor. The status quo raises broader issues about a major role for NATO in the Arctic which, until recently, has been firmly opposed by Canadian governments and reflects current beliefs that the Arctic should be an isolated theatre of cooperation dominated by the Arctic states, including Russia. Indeed, Canada vetoed the inclusion of an Arctic statement at the 2009 NATO summit held in Strasbourg-Kehl and the 2022 NATO Strategyic Concept refers to the high North—meaning the strategic Greenland-Iceland-United Kingdom (GIUK) North Atlantic gap—not the Arctic or the eastern approaches to North America.

Alongside these considerations, the threat environment of long-range cruise and hypersonic vehicles poses other significant implications on the intercept or defeat side of the equation. The probability that Canadian NORAD interceptors have the range to reach out and threaten the "archers" is likely low. With Russian launch points on the other side of the Arctic pole, this implies potential pre-emptive or offensive NORAD posturing, which has stability issues generally, and political ones for Canada. Of importance here, Canada has long kept offensive US plans as embodied in its Convential Prompt Strike at arm's length.

The long-range threat also indicates that NORAD is in the missile defence world, and this raises two issues for Canadian policy and NORAD. For now, Canada's commitment to the intercept side of the equation is limited to a new generation of short to long-range air-to-air missiles. While significant for confronting the cruise missile threat, whether these capabilities can deal with the hypersonic threat remains to seen. If so, however, such missiles would also likely have a potential low earth orbit anti-satellite capability, which would affect Canadian military space policy limited to the passive space defence side.

Effective interception requirements also raise the issue of whether Canada needs to invest in ground-based point defences (surface-to-air missiles) to deal with "leakers" for high valued targets in the South, and the NASS and Arctic forward operating locations. However, ground-based defences, in particular, raise the issue of Canada's non-participation in the US ground-based mid-course ballistic missile defence programme, especially given that the United States is moving forward with the integration of air and missile defence capabilities.[36] Currently, US continental ballistic defence is a USNORTHCOM mission, with NORAD and Canada on the outside looking in. Integration of air and missile defence, especially in the context of hypersonics, will likely affect NORAD's aerospace (air) control mission, and whether the distinction between air and ballistic missiles can be conceptually and operationally sustained remains to be seen.

Finally, all of these considerations also raise questions about the future of North American defence cooperation in the context of the under-developed tri-command relationship amongst Canadian Joint Operations Command (CJOC), NORAD and USNORTHCOM. Whether this overarching structure, especially in the context of a credible deterrence by denial posture, is the most efficient, effective or logical one is another open question. Of course, this also suggests the need to modernize the NORAD Agreement. Both Canada and the United States for now may not have an appetite to do so, but the fallout from the combination of the new threat environment and current technologically-driven modernization is likely to generate such a requirement.

Conclusion

The Canadian and American technologically-driven investment commitments to NORAD modernization are a vital first step. Even so, the policy implications of modernization, conveniently ignored in the NORAD modernization announcements, suggest a major transformation of NORAD is on the horizon. In some ways, they are reminiscent of the policy implications of initial Canadian-American air defence cooperation in the 1950s, which led to the creation of NORAD as a function of military requirements. In other words, NORAD modernization is much more than new infrastructure. It is about a much broader and deeper NORAD and thus an expanded and new continental defence relationship.

If the past is a guide, this will take place with little, if any, Canadian public debate about a "new" NORAD, as the government seeks to avoid the sensitive and feared issue of Canadian sovereignty relative to the United States. Nonetheless, it would be better if the government and DND go beyond simple funding announcements, as important as they are, to laying the groundwork for a well-informed public debate. If not, a future government may well face a defence-driven *fait accompli* with a domestic political firestorm likely to follow, albeit likely short-lived, as the Diefenbaker government did in 1958 following the signing of the NORAD agreement.

Time is pressing, and for the foreseeable future, North America and Canada will remain vulnerable to the threat posed by the new military technologies. This will affect how Canada and the United States respond to future international crises overseas—the persistent, preferred focus of both militaries.

Notes

1. Government of Canada (2017). "The North American Aerospace Defense Command (NORAD) illustrates the strength of our mutual commitment. United States and Canadian forces jointly conduct aerospace warning, aerospace control, and maritime warning in defense of North America. We will work to modernize and broaden our NORAD Partnership in these key domains, as well as in cyber and space."
2. Government of Canada (2019). "Continue Canada's ... work with the United States to ensure that the North American Aerospace Defence Command (NORAD) is modernized to meet existing and future challenges, as outlined in *Strong, Secure, Engaged*." This commitment was reiterated in the December Mandate letter to the new MND, Anita Anand following the fall election. See Government of Canada (2021c).
3. Government of Canada (2021a). In the statement, they also agreed that their respective Foreign and Defence Ministers would meet "in a 2+2 Ministerial format to further coordinate our joint contributions to collective security." Of note, there is no indication that such a meeting has occurred to date although the Permanent Joint Board on Defence met in 2021 and 2022.
4. CDAI (2021). A notable exception is the US Pathfinder Project to develop and employ Artificial Intelligence (AI) and machine learning to exploit the large volumes of surveillance data inputted into NORAD Headquarters and enhance information dominance and decision superiority. The specific date of Pathfinder's "launch" date is unclear.
5. Government of Canada (2021b, p. 289). Subsequently in January 2022, the government awarded a $592 million, seven-year contract for in service support of the North Warning System to the Inuit owned Nasittuq; effectively a life extension rather than modernization. See Department of National Defence (2022a).
6. Department of Defense (2021). "Modernize, improve, and better integrate the capabilities required for NORAD to maintain persistent awareness and understanding of potential threats to North America in the aerospace and maritime domains, to deter acts of aggression against North America, to respond to aerospace threats quickly and decisively when required, and to provide maritime warning consistent with the NORAD Agreement."
7. Government of Canada (2022a, p. 133).
8. Government of Canada (2022b). In the National Defence Fact Sheet released a month later, the $40 billion was reported as $38.6 billion on an accrual basis. See Department of National Defence (2022b).
9. Department of National Defence (2022b).
10. Government of Canada (2023).

11. With the 1981 renewal of the agreement, its terms of reference and its name changed from air to aerospace.
12. White House (1980). This strategy (Presidential Directive 59) stated: "If deterrence fails initially, we must be capable of fighting successfully so that the adversary would not achieve his war aims and would suffer costs that are or in any event greater than his gains, from having initiated an attack."
13. Charron and Fergusson (2022b, pp. 38–40).
14. Edmonstone (2018). The NWS cannot "see" as far as the new CADIZ and given the curvature of the earth, current ground-based radar cannot cope without connections to and augmentations from space-based and other emerging technologies. For a summary of events and consequences, see Edmonstone (2018).
15. Cruise missiles, due to their small radar cross-section and ground-hugging terrain mapping capability, cannot be easily tracked by traditional ground-based radars. Effective tracking requires a "look-down" capability available, for example, with over-the-horizon radars.
16. Sayler (2022).
17. White House (2022). Throughout the Cold War, the United States maintained a policy of nuclear first use. Although the US has not publicly adopted a no-first use policy, the recent US National Security Strategy in the context of its conventional military superiority has implicitly done so.
18. O'Shaughnessy and Fesler (2020).
19. Charron and Fergusson (2022a).
20. Of note, the new Arctic Offshore Patrol Ships (AOPS), with their first-year ice capability, do not possess a radar capable of contributing to the air warning and defence mission of NORAD. The Future Combat Ship, equipped with a variant of the Lockheed Martin Long Range Discrimination Radar, probably does have such a radar, but the vessel is not ice capable.
21. This has been reversed by a Canadian government on two occasions: Pierre Trudeau (1971) and Stephen Harper (2008) White Papers, but neither translated into a significant, long-term shifts in defence priorities.
22. Charron and Fergusson (2019).
23. The August 2021 Joint Statement only identifies four areas. The fifth, as discussed below, "future-proofing our capabilities to defend North America through investments in science and technology." See Department of National Defence (2022b).
24. On 4, 10, 11 and 12 February 2023, four air objects were shot down by NORAD over North America. See Gollom (2023). What was under-reported were 4 Russian planes that "buzzed" the Alaskan ADIZ on 14 February 2023. NORAD responded scrambling NORAD assigned interceptors as per normal.

25. The Arctic line is reminiscent of the 1950s Pinetree line. The extent of its coverage into the Arctic itself is unknown, as well as its potential ability to track cruise and hypersonic weapons that might "leak" through initial intercepts in the Arctic. Also, the location of the polar line is unspecified. It is unclear if it will follow the current location of NWS radars and/or include sites in the Canadian high Arctic archipelago.
26. Right now, the CAF is wholly dependent on the United States for air-to-air refueling. Canada's Strategic Tanker Transport Capability (STTC) project will replace the CC-150 Polaris fleet and enhance the RCAF's air mobility and air-to-air refuelling capacity eventually. The A330 Multi-Role Tanker Transport aircraft from Airbus Defence and Space of Madrid, Spain is the chosen replacement. This new fleet, named the CC-330 Husky, is estimated to have a life expectancy of thirty years.
27. Of note, investments are also underway to extend the life of the current NWS to 2035 and beyond.
28. Raytheon Company (2018). In 2018, Raytheon Canada received a contract to develop and test an over-the-horizon radar capable of dealing with Aurora Borealis interference in the high Arctic. The results of the tests are unclear. The Commander of NORAD and USNORTHCOM stated in testimony to the Armed Services committee on 8 March 2023 that "In order to maintain domain awareness and ensure integrated threat warning and attack assessment to national leadership, the United States and Canada must continue to move swiftly to field Over the Horizon Radar (OTHR), as funded in the FY23 Consolidated Omnibus Appropriations Act (P.L. 117–328). OTHR is a proven, affordable technology that will ensure our ability to detect threats from surface to space in the approaches to North America." VanHerck (2023, p. 10).
29. Regarding transportation capacity, the Arctic communities depend upon maritime re-supply during the shipping season, and thus new capacity will be required as well.
30. Compounding the process, DND and other involved government departments have constrained personnel resources, not least due to other major procurement projects stemming from the 2017 White Paper and 2018 Investment Plan.
31. Department of National Defence (2022a).
32. The exception here is the land domain not least of all because of political sensitivity in Canada related to sovereignty.
33. NORAD and USNORTHCOM (2021).
34. On 9/11, an American aircraft carrier off New York was transferred under NORAD command.
35. Several NATO allies have liaison officers at the NORAD and USNORTHCOM headquarters in Colorado Springs.

36. Government of Canada (2022b). At Trenton on 20 June 2022, Minister of National Defence Anand, in response to a question from the media, stated that Canadian policy had not changed, at least for the time being. The Chief of the Defence Staff Wayne Eyre, however, responded by raising US air and missile defence integration.

REFERENCES

Canadian Defence Associations Institute. 2021. *NORAD Modernization Forum: Information Dominance*. Nicholas Glesby (Rapporteur). Ottawa. Available at: https://cdainstitute.ca/norad-modernization-forum-info-dominance/.

Canadian Global Affairs Institute. 2022. *Implementing NORAD Modernization*. Defence Deconstructed Podcast. Available at: https://www.cgai.ca/implementing_norad_modernization.

Charron, Andrea, and James Fergusson. 2019. Out of Sight, Out of Mind NORAD vis-à-vis CANUS Politics. *Canadian Foreign Policy Journal* 26 (2): 137–151.

Charron, Andrea, and James Fergusson. 2022a. How to Strengthen Deterrence by Denial. *Strategic Studies Quarterly*: 42–58. Available at: https://www.airuniversity.af.edu/Portals/10/SSQ/documents/Volume-15_Issue-4/D-Charron.pdf.

Charron, Andrea and James Fergusson. 2022b. *NORAD: In Perpetuity and Beyond*. Montreal/Kingston: McGill Queen's University Press.

Department of Defense. 2021. *Joint Statement on NORAD Modernization*. Washington, DC: Government of the United States. Available at: https://www.defense.gov/News/Releases/Release/Article/2735041/joint-statement-on-norad-modernization/.

Department of National Defence. 2022a. Government of Canada Awards in-Service Support Contract for North Warning System. Available at: https://www.canada.ca/en/department-national-defence/news/2022/01/government-of-canada-awards-in-service-support-contract-for-north-warning-system.html.

Department of National Defence. 2022b. Fact Sheet: Funding for Continental Defence and NORAD Modernization. Ottawa. Available at: https://www.canada.ca/en/department-national-defence/services/operations/allies-partners/norad/facesheet-funding-norad-modernization.html.

Edmonstone, LCol Jody. 2018. *Canada's Expanded ADIZ*. Toronto: Canadian Forces College. Available at: https://www.cfc.forces.gc.ca/259/290/402/305/edmonstone.pdf.

Fergusson, James. 2022. North American Defence Modernization in an Uncertain Age. Macdonald-Laurier Institute Commentary. Available at: https://macdonaldlaurier.ca/north-american-defence-modernization-in-an-age-of-uncertainty/.

Gollom, Mark. 2023. Why Do Unidentified Objects Seem to be Popping Up Above North America All of a Sudden? CBC News. Available at: https://www.cbc.ca/news/world/unidentified-objects-norad-balloon-1.6746860.

Government of Canada. 2017. Joint Statement from President Donald J. Trump and Prime Minister Justin Trudeau. Ottawa. Available at: https://pm.gc.ca/en/news/statements/2017/02/13/joint-statement-president-donald-j-trump-and-prime-minister-justin.

Government of Canada. 2019. Mandate Letter to the Minister of National Defence. Ottawa. Available at: https://pm.gc.ca/en/mandate-letters/2019/12/13/archived-minister-national-defence-mandate-letter.

Government of Canada. 2021a. Roadmap for a Renewed US-Canada Partnership. Ottawa. Available at: https://pm.gc.ca/en/news/statements/2021/02/23/roadmap-renewed-us-canada-partnership.

Government of Canada. 2021b. Budget 2021: A Recovery Plan for Jobs, Growth and Resilience. Ottawa. Available at: https://www.budget.gc.ca/2021/home-accueil-en.html.

Government of Canada. 2021c. Mandate Letter to the Minister of National Defence. Ottawa. Available at: https://pm.gc.ca/en/mandate-letters/2021/12/16/minister-national-defence-mandate-letter.

Government of Canada. 2022a. Budget 2022: A Plan to Grow Our Economy and Make Life More Affordable. Ottawa. Available at: https://www.budget.canada.ca/2022/home-accueil-en.html.

Government of Canada. 2022b. Speech: Minister of National Defence Announces Canada's NORAD Modernization Plan. Available at: https://www.canada.ca/en/department-national-defence/news/2022/06/minister-of-national-defence-announces-canadas-norad-modernization-plan.html and https://www.youtube.com/watch?v=OV8EgE2_F5A.

Government of Canada. 2023. NORAD Modernization Timelines. Available at: https://www.canada.ca/en/department-national-defence/services/operations/allies-partners/norad/norad-modernization-project-timelines.html.

NORAD and USNORTHCOM 2021. Commander NORAD and USNORTHCOM Releases Strategic Vision. Available at: https://www.norad.mil/Francais/Article/2537173/commander-norad-and-usnorthcom-releases-strategic-vision/.

O'Shaughnessy, Terrence J., and Peter M. Fesler. 2020. *Hardening the Shield: A Credible Deterrent & Capable Defense for North America*. Washington,

DC: Canada Institute. Available at: https://www.wilsoncenter.org/sites/def
ault/files/media/uploads/documents/Hardening%20the%20Shield_A%20C
redible%20Deterrent%20%26%20Capable%20Defense%20for%20North%20A
merica_EN.pdf.
Pugliese, David. 2022. Canada Plans New $1-Billion Radar to Protect North American Cities. *Ottawa Citizen.* Available at: https://ottawacitizen.com/news/local-news/canada-plans-new-1-billion-radar-to-protect-north-ame rican-cities.
Raytheon Company. 2018. Raytheon Building Canadian Radar to Test Effects of Aurora Borealis. Available at: https://www.newswire.ca/news-releases/ray theon-building-canadian-radar-to-test-effects-of-aurora-borealis-701865451. html.
Sayler, Kelly M. 2022. *Hypersonic Weapons: Background and Issues for Congress.* Washington, DC: Congressional Research Services. Available at: https://sgp. fas.org/crs/weapons/R45811.pdf.
VanHerck, General Glen D. 2023. Statement of General Glen D. VanHerck, US Airforce Commander USNORTHCOM and NORAD Before the House Armed Services Committee. Available at: https://armedservices.house.gov/sites/republicans.armedservices.house.gov/files/03.08.23%20VanHerck%20S tatement.pdf.
White House. 1980. Presidential Directive/NSC 59. Available at: https://www.jimmycarterlibrary.gov/assets/documents/directives/pd59.pdf.
White House. 2022. US National Security Strategy. Available at: https://www.whitehouse.gov/wp-content/uploads/2022/10/Biden-Harris-Administrati ons-National-Security-Strategy-10.2022.pdf.

Canada's Defence Policy Trade-Offs

Stéfanie von Hlatky and Srdjan Vucetic

Russia's re-invasion of Ukraine in 2022 has changed the shape of defence policy discussions everywhere, leading many countries to increase military spending. Like other NATO and G7 countries, Canada moved to support the Ukrainian military with arms transfers, such as anti-tank weapon systems, as well as various other forms of aid, including sanctions targeting Kremlin assets.[1] The war, and its implications for the broader security environment, has also accelerated calls for an update of the last defence policy, *Strong, Secure, Engaged* (SSE), released in 2017.[2] In fact, the rise in strategic competition culminating in a large-scale conventional

---

For comments and criticisms, we thank Kerry Buck, David Haglund, Adam MacDonald, and the editors of this volume. All errors remain ours.

S. von Hlatky
Department of Political Studies, Queen's University, Kingston, ON, Canada

S. Vucetic (✉)
Graduate School of Public and International Affairs, University of Ottawa, Ottawa, ON, Canada
e-mail: Srdjan.Vucetic@uottawa.ca

© The Author(s), under exclusive license to Springer Nature Switzerland AG 2023
T. Juneau and P. Lagassé (eds.), *Canadian Defence Policy in Theory and Practice, Volume 2*, Canada and International Affairs, https://doi.org/10.1007/978-3-031-37542-2_6

war on the European continent should lead to more regular reassessments of foreign and defence policy, as is done in the United States (US) through the quadrennial defence review process. Given the assorted risks and threats Canada already faces or could very soon face—another war, another pandemic, assorted effects of the climate crisis—questions of defence are only a small piece of the overall puzzle. Yet they must be revisited cyclically, rather than relying on an ad hoc approach to major policy updates.[3] Any government would be daunted by the idea of launching—and then maintaining and managing—such periodic reviews, especially given the many institutional and political challenges involved (see the chapter by Juneau and Rigby in this volume).

But such reviews are driven by one of the top challenges of Canadian policymaking in general: assessing defence issues in their totality and improving Canada's own ability to tackle them, whether on its own or in close cooperation with allies. While we acknowledge that integrated threat analysis is difficult business because of intra- and inter-governmental silos, it is necessary to invest in that capacity. From the perspective of the Department of National Defence (DND) and the Canadian Armed Forces (CAF), this intent has already been captured in the Pan-Domain Force Employment Concept, a document that acknowledges the proliferation of threats across domains and the requirement of building closer coordination between government departments, but also externally with civil society. Policymakers in Ottawa have always worked hard at aligning Canada's goals and commitments with necessarily limited resources and capabilities. Today they must work even harder.

Our chapter makes two prescriptions, one more conceptual and one more substantive. Our starting premise is the idea that governments cannot successfully navigate a tumultuous geopolitical environment without a strategic vision or guidance for the country. To that end, we propose a conceptual framework which summarizes the domestic and international factors that should support such dialogue.

The other prescription we make is more substantive: given past tendencies to overpromise and under-deliver in defence, Canada and Canadians should be more decisive and more pragmatic in identifying Canada's strategic opportunities and constraints. Here, too, conceptual frameworks are important: while they cannot "solve" policy trade-offs, they can at least help blunt the sharpest edges of those trade-offs.

To make these prescriptions concrete at the outset, let us consider the shifts in the security context following Russia's full-scale invasion of

Ukraine in 2022. From a Canadian perspective, the first challenge was to adapt to the war, as NATO reinforced its deterrence against Russia and overall defence posture, while also affirming its open-door policy with respect to Sweden and Finland as members. But NATO also revised its Strategic Concept to better reflect the challenges posed by China and climate change. Accordingly, Canadian leaders made ample policy announcements that year, nodding in the direction of a new defence review update originally meant to be released in 2023.

We can safely assume this document—if or when it is released—will address renewed NATO commitments and Canada's recent Indo-Pacific strategy. It will also say something meaningful about NORAD and North American continental defence—the so-called missing chapter of SSE—and the necessity of modernizing the defence ministry machinery. Welcome as it is, we think this update should be seen as only the first step towards a proper review of Canada's international policy writ large. This entails attention to everything from increasing the country's diplomatic footprint to addressing various "feminist" foreign policy inconsistencies to the most recent "doctrinal" statements, namely those by Foreign Minister Joly on China as a disruptive power, Deputy Prime Minister Freeland on friend-shoring, and Minister of Innovation, Science, and Industry Champagne on decoupling.[4]

Relatedly, we think the defence policy update is unlikely to *dramatically* increase Canada's defence spending—even if this spending has been on an upward trajectory since SSE. An honest and pragmatic consideration of policy trade-offs would therefore lead to a strategic allocation of resources that permits the CAF to (1) maintain its *core* functions, such as training, recruitment, and retention (see the chapter by Goldenberg and Otis), *and* (2) carry out overseas deployment of *one* fighter jet squadron and/or *one* fully operational brigade. We think achieving both would constitute enormous success in terms of dealing with policy trade-offs. Conversely, expecting more than that only increases the risk of reverting to the self-inflicted problem of "trying to do too much with too little", without a clear articulation of how these commitments further Canadian foreign and defence policy priorities.

Strategic Competition Today

Parallels between Ukraine and the early days of the Cold War are incredibly tempting. Then, as now, collective defence and deterrence together formed one of the core pillars of the NATO alliance, with the regime in the Kremlin identified as the most acute direct threat.[5] The 2022 NATO Strategic Concept says this explicitly: "The Russian Federation is the most significant and direct threat to Allies' security and to peace and stability in the Euro-Atlantic area. It seeks to establish spheres of influence and direct control through coercion, subversion, aggression and annexation".[6]

Useful as they often are, broad historical comparisons can obfuscate some key aspects of today's strategic competition, to use a currently popular term. To begin with, in contrast to the Cold War, today's geopolitical struggles take place in the context of (lingering) globalized interdependence and (expanding) US-China decoupling. China's spectacular growth—and the so-called rise of the Rest more generally—has in large part been a function of the former condition, meaning of rising global trade and investment plus capital-market access together with the massive transfer of Western technological (and legal) know-how. This world—some called it neoliberal globalization—is now gone. Replacing it is a world of national security considerations, many of them zero-sum. This in turn means more restrictions on market access in key sectors of the economy, more export controls, and a real prospect of all-out technology and trade wars.

Foreign and defence policies everywhere will take time to adjust to this deglobalizing world. The most dramatic shift has been in Putin's Russia. But China, too, under President Xi Jinping, has become more militarized and more militaristic—witness the dramatic nuclear, conventional, and "new technologies" warfare buildups, the assorted territorial feuds with India, Vietnam, and other neighbours, and, indeed, the ignoble hostage diplomacy against Canada. Combine these trends with the considerable reach and attractiveness of its vaunted Belt and Road Initiative and a sanctioned Russia moving closer to China (not just in energy transactions but also in terms of participation in a renminbi-based finance and payments systems), and one might be tempted to conclude that China's "hegemonic *potential*" far exceeds that of the Soviet Union at its height, in the late 1960s.[7]

The so-called West has responded to these shifts with talk of decoupling, or its corollary friendshoring. For many, all this evidence is of movement towards a "bipolar", "multipolar" or, indeed, "multi-order world".[8] In this view, the future will belong to regional power blocs in supply chains, in regulation, and in technological and financial infrastructure. Will this world generate an existential, Cold War-style competition? Here we must keep several points of difference in mind. To begin with, decoupling briefs well, but it is much harder to implement, as the energy crisis brought on by Russia's assault on Ukraine demonstrates. Relatedly, both the West and China regard climate as one area which cannot be decoupled.[9] Next, even if each power bloc ends up developing, and operating on, its own set rules, these rules need not evolve into fully formed, ideologically distinct, and mutually exclusive international ordering projects that characterized the Cold War. In contrast to its Soviet predecessor, the current "China model" stands in cultural and ideological opposition to the idea and practice of liberal democracy but not necessarily to capitalism—even if the latter must be qualified with adjectives, as in "state capitalism", "party-state capitalism", and "authoritarian capitalism". Perhaps this will change, but in the foreseeable future, it is hard to imagine a post-capitalist China model that successfully reconciles growth with authoritarian governance.

But is China a larger, longer-term threat to Canada and its allies than right-wing radicalism? In addition to being a popular academic exam question these days, this is also a key question for Canadian strategists. In the United States, a radicalized Republican Party continues to champion "Trumpist" policies and discourses, which in turn resonate with a number of political movements, parties, and leaders in Asia, Africa, Europe, and South America. The consequences of these political and ideological struggles affect Canadian defence considerations in some fundamental ways, whether in terms of civil-military relations or in terms of the standard Canadian defence questions—the scope and intensity of NATO commitments or Canada's status in the continental defence system.[10]

The fact that Canadian defence reviews must fit a particular diplomatic decorum means that "Trumpism" (or some equivalent) is unlikely to ever be mentioned, let alone configured as a principal threat.[11] But if Ottawa is to cyclically re-evaluate its defence posture based on iterative assessments of all threats, it must establish an analytical framework for asking (if not directly answering) even the most undiplomatic of questions. More importantly, Ottawa must be disciplined in applying this framework to policy. This way policymakers can be more responsive—rather than "merely" reactive—in adjusting the nation's strategic orientation and planning for appropriate capabilities as a result.

Conceptualizing Trade-Offs

Foreign policy magazines are full of advice on strategy. In a recent essay, Rodrik and Walt suggest that the path to designing a more benign international order entails recognizing that it is best to compartmentalize issues to achieve progress. Though their focus is on great and major powers, the framework they offer suggests that tackling international challenges need not fall prey to a "conflict vs. cooperation" dichotomy but should instead be categorized and addressed based on the likelihood of achieving agreement. This leads to asking a pragmatic set of questions to steer states' strategies of diplomatic engagement, like identifying "actions that should be prohibited outright", from issues where "compromises or adjustments would be feasible and mutually beneficial" (2022, p. 155).

As a self-identified middle power, Canada does not have the leverage that major and great powers have in terms of identifying challenges that are ripe for great power compromise, nor can it decisively influence strategic outcomes along the cooperation-competition spectrum. What Canada can do, however, is to be clear-headed about the foreign and defence policy choices it is faced with, along with the trade-offs that necessarily follow. Though designed with the Indo-Pacific context in mind, the framework developed by MacDonald and Vance (2021) is particularly instructive in this regard.[12] It not only identifies the range of strategic postures that Canada could adopt in the region, but it also considers how geopolitical assumptions impact those respective postures. So, if Canada opts for minimal defence engagement in the Indo-Pacific, a position we favour, it would likely be on the basis of strategic uncertainty vis-à-vis China and the US's global leadership potential, combined with the likelihood that Canada's like-minded partners would not pick up the slack. By considering Canada's options in the Indo-Pacific alongside geopolitical assumptions which are mostly outside of its control, one can achieve a more systematic analysis of the foreign and defence policy trade-offs Ottawa is likely to face in defining and executing its new Indo-Pacific strategy.

Building on this literature, we propose a simple analytical framework that seeks to bring more clarity to a range of factors that define the boundaries of decision-making and policymaking in the realm of defence.

What our framework adds is a logic of domestic political and military constraints, as these enable or impair Ottawa's strategic ambitions. In other words, rather than privileging the international over the domestic, or vice-versa, we find there is analytical purchase in integrating factors at both domestic and international "levels", so to speak.[13] This yields a matrix sketched out in Fig. 1. There we integrate the threat environment and alliance demands, factors which operate predominantly on a regional or international level, with more domestic-level factors tied to the political environment and military capabilities.

Our assessment in the upper left corner configures US unpredictability as a more acute and immediate concern to Canadian interests than strategic competition with China and Russia. This means that Canada's response to China and Russia will be assessed through the prism of its bilateral relationship with the United States. Whether due to right-wing radicalism or sheer US unpredictability, Canada's special bilateral

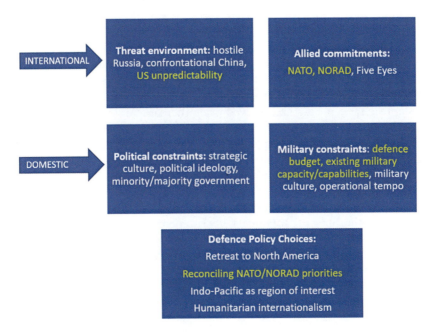

Fig. 1 Opportunities/constraints

continental relationship is vulnerable to swings in the US political landscape because Canada's economic dependence on the United States is simultaneously dependence on "normal" US politics, meaning on stable regulation, rule of law, working capital markets, and other drivers of trade and investment. Moreover, right-wing populism, an aspect of US unpredictability, can affect the defence equation by undermining the political consensus that has traditionally supported the US-based alliance system, from NATO to American defence pacts in the Indo-Pacific.

In terms of allied commitments, defence investments in support of NATO and NORAD objectives can help Canada better manage its defence relationship with the United States by simultaneously having close access to US military structures through sustained binational defence cooperation but with a solid counterweight in Europe. While North American defence, with NORAD at its core, and the NATO command structure, are distinct entities, it is clear that developing a more networked system between these two poles will serve Canadian interests. The Five Eyes network is important too, particularly now that it has been expanded across the security domain. But it is still not as far-reaching, in addition to lacking a clear regional focus.

When it comes to domestic politics and how this consideration might affect defence policy, the right-left cleavage is not as stark as it might be in other countries. Past experience also shows that foreign policy compromises can easily be achieved when there is a minority government. Barring a defence policy orientation that would represent a major clash with Canada's dominant strategic culture (or cultures), decision-makers in Ottawa enjoy considerable political latitude domestically. However, some options are foreclosed by international constraints. Humanitarian internationalism might be the preferred option of the Liberals and/or NDP, but making it the cornerstone of Canada's foreign and defence policy is not feasible in the current geopolitical environment.

Conversely, military constraints have a great impact on the range of defence policy choices that Ottawa faces. While Canada has reduced its operational tempo in the Middle East and Africa, there is pressure to prioritize its limited resources through NATO and NORAD both because of the threat environment and existing allied commitments and demands. In the CAF, we acknowledge that culture change is a major undertaking and certainly impacts the way the organization functions, but we reject the view that it might detract attention from existing defence commitments. Rather, the recruitment and retention challenges that the CAF is facing in a competitive labour market, as well as long periods of under-investments in defence, are the more significant constraints on Canadian defence policy.

CHOICES AND CAPABILITIES

With the above framework in mind, we can now revisit our opening discussion about meeting national goals, allied expectations, and unpredictable global threats. First, while we think Cold War analogies are misleading, we also think that Canada's geostrategic interests clearly lie with its traditional Cold War-era allies and partners—with the United States and the rest of NATO, with the Five Eyes partners Australia and New Zealand, as well as with Japan and South Korea. Security, intelligence, and defence relationships with these "like-minded" countries will likely continue to deepen in the foreseeable future—whatever the rhetorical status of a trope of a global contest between democracies and autocracies.[14]

Next, the war in Ukraine has forced Canada's hand in narrowing its strategic focus. It already had skin in the game by leading a NATO multinational battlegroup in Latvia, through enhanced Forward Presence (eFP), but also in terms of its bilateral training activities with Ukraine after the annexation of Crimea. NATO will ask Canada to double down on its commitment to bolster deterrence and defence on the Eastern Flank.

Meanwhile, the Indo-Pacific is more important than ever and has made its way onto the transatlantic agenda, as reflected in the 2022 NATO Strategic Concept: "The People's Republic of China's (PRC) stated ambitions and coercive policies challenge our interests, security and values".[15] Note that NATO falls short of explicitly identifying Beijing as a threat. Although the US government often uses stronger language, it is unlikely to put additional pressure on Canada in the short term to do more on defence in the Indo-Pacific. The Pentagon's 2022 National Defence Strategy, for example, names Japan, Australia, and South Korea as the key allies for deterring China in the region; Canada, in contrast, is mentioned only in North America and the Arctic (NDS 2022, pp. 14–15, cf 10, 16).[16] Prima facie, such small details matter a lot because they add to the argument that Canada need not jump into US-led confrontation with China just yet. But the same argument follows from our framework, too. In the short to medium term, Beijing is unlikely to achieve regional hegemony and Canadian politics is unlikely to decenter itself from Ontario and

Quebec. Accordingly, we see neither political nor geopolitical reasons for a complex and costly "pivot" away from the Euro-Atlantic, even if other like-minded countries, like the United States, have already started to do so in terms of their long-term strategic orientations.

On this point, we wish to be clear: the government in Ottawa *should* implement its Indo-Pacific strategy, which supports Royal Canadian Navy deployments to the region, primarily for the purpose of keeping up with allied military exercises and training. Beyond that, the choice for Canada is to narrow the scope of its Indo-Pacific engagement to developing economic and diplomatic ties. So, while some heat and light have been expended on why Canada should seek to join AUKUS and/or the Quad[17]—to name but two new security institutions whose strategic raison d'être is China—we think the best course of action is serious investment in state capacity *and* in legacy institutions and networks. Moreover, NATO offers Canada a convenient multilateral platform that is unparalleled in other regions of interest, because it has been reinforced over decades. Deeper military engagement in the Indo-Pacific can and should wait, at least until the diplomatic and economic presence is on stronger footing. Continuing to invest in defence diplomacy is a sound compromise option too.

The United States spending more time and attention on the Indo-Pacific, and its strategic rivalry with China in particular, would strengthen the argument calling on Canada to solidify its NATO ties and to bolster the North American presence in the transatlantic equation. The greatest American pressure will be for investments in North American continental defence, both for the renewal of NORAD infrastructure and for the implementation of a more defence-oriented Arctic Strategy. Canada's latest defence budget increases have been earmarked for that purpose and Ottawa will not be able to resist additional pressures coming from Washington to pony up money and resources for continental defence.

On this point, too, we must be clear: the 2022 midterm election in the United States notwithstanding, Canada is *also* facing more uncertainty when it comes to its bilateral relationship with its southern neighbour. Political instability and the rise of far-right extremism, perhaps best exemplified by the January 6 insurrection, should lead Canada to embed North American security contributions in the broader transatlantic security equation. (And this should go above and beyond the traditional alliance pressures Canada has always faced.) This necessarily entails ending Ottawa's obstruction to a transatlantic dialogue on Arctic Security. In

August 2022, when the NATO Secretary General visited Canada, with a tour of its facilities in the High North, we observed that this shift was indeed taking place. In terms of NATO diplomacy, Canada will need to be more assertive in advocating the importance of the Alliance's Western and Northern flanks, which receive much less attention than its Eastern and Southern flanks. This will be an important shift for Canada, which is not used to pressing other allies in Brussels in favour of its own geopolitical interests. The fact that Montréal was chosen as the host city for the new NATO Centre of Excellence on Climate Change and Security, for example, simultaneously advances Canadian interests in multilateralism, in knowledge and practices for climate adaptation, and in the ongoing efforts to build stronger national (and North American) presence in an increasingly accessible Arctic.

Narrowing the analytical boundaries of defence policy trade-offs, as proposed in our framework, allows us to identify the centre of gravity for Canadian defence policy, when compared to other priorities. The framework also leads us to better appreciate the logics which connect international and domestic factors to produce a more definite strategic orientation to guide DND/CAF stakeholders. And then comes the question of capabilities. The Liberal government insists on its commitment to what its ministers refer to as the long-term, multi-year approach to national defence. This logically necessitates updates to policy, namely that outlined in SSE, as well as additional funding, such as the nearly $5 billion earmarked for a replacement of the North Warning System and other NORAD modernization efforts. This is crucial, for SSE very clearly promises to deter and defend "sea lines of communication and maritime approaches to Allied territory in the North Atlantic", with an eye on Russia.[18]

Successive federal governments will be compelled to sustain these and other investments to build military capacities. In terms of major conventional weapons systems, the CAF will receive new Arctic offshore patrol ships (two have been delivered), new surface combatants, new fighter jets, and new radar, satellite, and sensor assets for a more advanced NORAD. Canada likewise requires new armoured vehicles in the form of both Light Armoured Vehicles (LAVs) and tanks as well as new capabilities in air defence, electronic warfare, and long-range firepower. All these systems of course come with new infrastructure and new training programs—and so with a degree of inter-service competition.[19]

With the war in Ukraine ongoing, Canada's near-term focus should be on what it can contribute to NATO's eastern flank: one fighter jet squadron and one capable, operational brigade. This of course requires addressing major shortfalls in strategic airlift but also means sustaining some old gaps, not least with respect to the Royal Canadian Navy (RCN). This, once again, is in the very character of strategy. Differently put, the point of good security and defence preparedness for Canada is making the best of the available resources at home, while also using alliances and partnership to deter threats and manage risks.

Looking beyond the 2020s, there is a doubtless need for constant investment towards "new" military capacities and contributions, especially in light of new cyber threats, advanced hypersonic weaponry and robotics, artificial intelligence, quantum computing, and assorted military technologies that few could foresee a decade ago. But here, too, tough choices will have to be made. Rather than obsessing about all new technologies that have military value, the federal government should pursue those that are most likely to benefit Canada's traditional defence needs. An Arctic detection system for semi-autonomous undersea vehicles makes strategic sense. A fleet of nuclear-powered submarines does not.

Like defence commitments, national conversations on strategy require sustained political follow-through. The last comprehensive review of national security policy was completed in 2004—a fact that some cite as evidence of a certain complacency that characterizes both the governors and the governed.[20] Yet, polling done during the first year of the Ukraine war shows the Canadian public wants a Canada that is willing and able to stand united with its allies, and NATO allies in particular. Perhaps the governed are signalling they want to pay for a stronger state and a more active foreign policy? The governors should take heed of both continuities and changes in these signals (for further context, see Boucher 2021).

Conclusion

A rising strategic competition between China and the US-led West compounds the economic challenges wrought by the war in Ukraine, the COVID-19 pandemic and the accelerating effects of climate change. Like many other US allies, Canada has restricted commercial exchanges with China, some of it in retaliation to the latter's human rights abuses at home. Beijing has reciprocated in kind, but with an eye on increasing capacity for self-reliance in technology and science. Beijing has also supported Moscow over Ukraine, touting the end of US hegemony era and the arrival of a multipolar world order—a strategic goal the Chinese and Russian leaderships have shared since 1997.

Whatever the next iteration of such zero-sum games, Canada's values and interests remain most closely aligned with its traditional allies and partners. This alignment likewise determines the order of geostrategic priorities and military posture. In practice, this means NORAD and NATO remain the starting point for defence policy updates. So, even though successive governments in Ottawa may come to agree that an assertive China constitutes the greatest long-term threat to Canada, the strategic imperative should be on the Atlantic and Arctic regions, given the need for prioritization. The Canadian military is likely to more efficiently and effectively respond to threats and risks closer to home than by long-distance naval power projection in the South China Sea.

Reflections on strategy are always shaped by a specific yet evolving political and geopolitical context, with factors which our proposed framework captures. This compounds the main challenge for those proffering advice: when to advocate for staying the strategic course as opposed to for change. Canadian policymakers should no doubt continue to study the war in Ukraine and keep distilling its lessons learned, while also looking across the Pacific to China. But this should always be done with the understanding that the core of Canada's security capacity is vested in the transatlantic area.

Notes

1. Government of Canada (2022).
2. Department of National Defence (2017).
3. Buck and Manulak (2022) and Chase (2022).
4. Réseau d'analyse stratégique (2022).
5. Spencer (1951).
6. NATO (2022, p. 4).
7. We emphasize the qualifier potential. Vucetic (2019, 2022a).
8. Rodrik and Walt (2022) and Flockhart and Korosteleva (2022).
9. In other words, while strategic competition with China will continue to disrupt trading patterns and supply chains, these, plus health and science, are areas likely to remain protected (Réseau d'analyse stratégique 2022).
10. Rigby and Juneau (2022).
11. It is also unlikely to be mentioned in the same paragraph, for in this genre of writing the political and ideological contestation between the

rival positions in advanced capitalist democracies is conceptually separate from China's rise or Russia's revanchism. For further consideration, see Note 1 and the literature cited therein.
12. NATO (2022).
13. Surveying the Canadian foreign and defence policy literature further, we see a fairly broad consensus among scholars about the need to combine different domestic and international-level factors to guide analyses on Canada's strategic options, major foreign policy decisions, and commitments to allied operations. As a sample, see von Hlatky (2013), Auerswald and Saideman (2014), and Juneau et al. (2020).
14. See again Buck and Manulak (2022). For an attempt at assessing "like-mindedness" empirically, see Vucetic and Ramadanovic (2019).
15. NATO (2022, p. 5).
16. National Defense Strategy of the United States (2022, pp. 10, 16).
17. For some light on the former, see Haglund and Nicol (2023) and Carvin and Juneau (2023).
18. Department of National Defence (2017, p. 92).
19. The surface combatants and fighter jets most clearly underscore the continuing importance of "seamless" or "advanced" interoperability with US armed forces in Canadian force development. See, respectively, Choi (2021) and Vucetic (2022b).
20. Rigby and Juneau (2022, p. 3).

References

Auerswald, David P., and Stephen M. Saideman. 2014. *NATO in Afghanistan: Fighting Together, Fighting Alone*. Princeton: Princeton University Press.

Boucher, Jean-Christophe. 2021. Opinion publique et politique de défense du Canada à l'ombre de la compétition des grandes puissances. *Études canadiennes/Canadian Studies* 91: 33–62.

Buck, Kerry, and Michael W. Manulak. 2022. Friend-Shoring Canada's Foreign Policy? *Policy*. Available at https://www.policymagazine.ca/friend-shoring-canadas-foreign-policy/.

Carvin, Stephanie and Thomas Juneau. 2023. Why AUKUS and Not CAUKUS? It's a Polach, not a Party. In Srdjan Vucetic, ed. AUKUS Among Democracies, *International Journal*. OnlineFirst https://journals.sagepub.com/home/ijx

Chase, Steven. 2022. Time for Western 'Decoupling' from China and Other Authoritarian States, Says Innovation Minister. *The Globe and Mail*. Available at https://www.theglobeandmail.com/politics/article-canada-trade-china-authoritarian-countries-champagne/.

Choi, Timothy. 2021. What Can We Expect from the New Canadian Surface Combatant? CDA Institute. Available at https://cdainstitute.ca/timothy-choi-what-can-we-expect-from-the-new-csc-combat-ships/.

Flockhart, T., and E.A. Korosteleva. 2022. War in Ukraine: Putin and the Multi-order World. *Contemporary Security Policy* 43 (3): 1–16.

Government of Canada. 2022. Canada's Response to the Russian Invasion of Ukraine. Available at https://www.international.gc.ca/world-monde/issues_development-enjeux_developpement/response_conflict-reponse_conflits/crisis-crises/ukraine.aspx?lang=eng.

Government of Canada, Department of National Defence. 2017. Strong, Secure, Engaged: Canada's Defence Policy. Available at https://www.canada.ca/en/department-national-defence/corporate/reports-publications/canada-defence-policy.html/.

Government of the United States of America. 2022. National Defense Strategy. Available at https://media.defense.gov/2022/Oct/27/2003103845/-1/-1/1/2022-NATIONAL-DEFENSE-STRATEGY-NPR-MDR.PDF.

Haglund, David G., and Wesley Nicol. 2023. Mirror, Mirror, on the Wall: AUKUS and the Question of a "Special" Canada-US Defence Relationship. In *History Has Made Us Friends: Reflections on the "Special" Relationship between Canada and the United States* eds. Donald E. Abelson and Stephen Brooks, Montreal and Kingston: McGill-Queen's University Press.

Juneau, Thomas, Philippe Lagassé, and Srdjan Vucetic, eds. 2020. *Canadian Defence Policy in Theory and Practice*. Cham: Palgrave Macmillan.

MacDonald, Adam, and Carter Vance. 2021. Developing a Canadian Indo-Pacific Geopolitical Orientation. *International Journal* 76 (4): 564–593.

NATO, Strategic Concept. 2022. Available at https://www.nato.int/strategic-concept.

Réseau d'analyse stratégique. 2022. Par dessein plutôt que par défaut: Établir un leadership mondial inclusif soutenu par des capacités de défense ciblées. Available at https://ras-nsa.ca/wp-content/uploads/2022/09/RAPPORT-RAS-FR.pdf.

Rigby, Vincent, and Thomas Juneau. 2022. A National Security Strategy for the 2020s. GSPIA Policy Report, Ottawa. Available at https://socialsciences.uottawa.ca/public-international-affairs/sites/socialsciences.uottawa.ca.public-international-affairs/files/natsec_report_gspia_may2022.pdf.

Rodrik, Dani, and Stephen M. Walt. 2022. How to Build a Better Order: Limiting Great Power Rivalry in an Anarchic World. *Foreign Affairs*: 142–155.

Spencer, R.A. 1951. *Canada in World Affairs, 1946–1949, from UN to NATO*, vol. V. Toronto: Canadian Institute of International Affairs.

von Hlatky, Stéfanie. 2013. *American Allies in Times of War: The Great Asymmetry*. Oxford: Oxford University Press.

Vucetic, Srdjan. 2019. Chinese Counter-Hegemony? Evidence from 'Making Identity Count.' In *America's Allies and the Decline of US Hegemony*, ed. Justin Massie and Jonathan Paquin, 43–57. Oxon and New York: Routledge.

Vucetic, Srdjan. 2022a. China and Its Region: An Assessment of Hegemonic Prospects. *Journal of Regional Security* 16 (2): 127–150.

Vucetic, Srdjan. 2022b. More Defence Funding in Wake of Canada's F-35 About-Face. The Conversation. Available at https://theconversation.com/federal-budget-2022-more-defence-funding-in-wake-of-canadas-f-35-about-face-180552.

Vucetic, Srdjan, and Bojan Ramadanovic. 2019. Canada in the United Nations General Assembly from Trudeau to Trudeau. *Canadian Journal of Political Science* 53 (1): 79–98.

The Defence Budget

Dave Perry

In June 2017, then Minister of National Defence Harjit Singh announced a defence policy promising to keep Canada "Strong at home…Secure in North America…and Engaged in the world."[1] *Strong Secure Engaged* (SSE) was an ambitious defence policy, with 132 itemized initiatives, underpinned by a twenty year funding model. The second sentence of the Minister's cover letter to the policy noted "Strong, Secure, Engaged is a long-term, fully funded plan built around people," emphasizing the centrality of fiscal and human resources to the policy. While chapters by Mackenzie and Goldenberg address the human resources issues with SSE, this chapter will assess the fiscal basis of the policy over its first five years and track the evolution of defence funding since 2017. In short, the overall defence spending increase promised in SSE is being met, and there has been real growth in spending across the three major components of defence spend since 2017. However, long-standing difficulties spending funds for Capital procurement have continued resulting in significantly less capital spending than compared to the extraordinarily

D. Perry (✉)
Canadian Global Affairs Institute, Ottawa, ON, Canada
e-mail: dperry@cgai.ca

© The Author(s), under exclusive license to Springer Nature Switzerland AG 2023
T. Juneau and P. Lagassé (eds.), *Canadian Defence Policy in Theory and Practice, Volume 2,* Canada and International Affairs,
https://doi.org/10.1007/978-3-031-37542-2_7

ambitious plans outlined in SSE. Following Russia's further invasion of Ukraine in February 2022, substantial new funding has been added to defence. Much of that has been devoted to capital, so it remains to be seen how much Canada's defence fiscal trajectory will change, absent major changes to Canada's acquisition of capital equipment and infrastructure.

Defence Budgeting and Spending in Canada

Canada's fiscal process has three distinct aspects: budgets; allocations; and spending. The budget for the Department of National Defence and the Canadian Armed Forces is established as part of the Government of Canada's overall budgeting process which sets funding aside in Canada's fiscal framework, thereby establishing the maximum impact of defence on the government of Canada's fiscal position. To actually use the funds set aside in the fiscal framework, they are allocated to departments through the Estimates, which is "the process by which the government asks Parliament to appropriate funds in support of approved programs and services."[2] Departments then spend their allocations according to plans itemized at a high level in the Departmental Plan and according to more detailed business plans for the constituent components of the DND/CAF such as the three military services. The actual spending that occurs is reported in the Public Accounts of Canada. To sum up, the federal budget process provides funds for DND which must then be allocated to the department annually, and then DND must then actually spend its allocation. Since the late 2000s, actually spending the funds available to defence has been problematic for the component of the defence budget devoted to capital. As outlined below, since the publication of SSE, Canada has been successful at spending the total amount of money anticipated on defence, but has significantly underspent the amount of money devoted to capital investments.

The three main categories of defence allocation and spending are personnel, operations and maintenance (O&M), and capital. Personnel encompasses the human resources component of defence, the majority of which are uniformed troops. Capital is the cost of acquiring new assets, the majority of which is equipment, and O&M which encompasses all of the costs of running the defence organization, and the organization's readiness to conduct operations.[3]

Especially important for defence, given the large share of its spending on capital equipment and infrastructure, Canada's budgeting process uses accrual accounting rules, whereas both allocations and spending use a modified cash basis of accounting. Under cash accounting rules, all spending is recorded in the year it occurs. Under accrual accounting practices, however, the budgetary impact of capital costs is amortized, or spread out, over a long-term depreciation schedule that stretches over decades, irrespective of the year in which spending occurs. These depreciation schedules can span up to 25 years for military vehicles, 30 years for arms and weapons, 35 years for ships, 40 years for aircraft, and 80 years for works and infrastructure.[4]

Since 2017, the Capital Investment Fund (CIF) is the source of funds that defence uses to make capital purchases.[5] It is a special allotment of the fiscal framework set aside specifically to account for the depreciation of defence capital assets that stretches over multiple decades beyond the twenty years over which defence policy budgets are now normally communicated. Enabled by a Capability Investment Program Plan Review (CIPPR) decision aid that uses inputs, including the priorities of each capability sponsor, DND/CAF wide priorities, and national policy direction, defence identifies a portfolio of capabilities that makes best use of the money available in the CIF.[6] Importantly, this process evaluates not just what capabilities will be acquired, but *when* those capabilities will be acquired by sequencing the depreciation schedules for the capital assets in the defence capital investment plan over time.

Since the depreciation of a capital asset does not begin until the asset is accepted, any delays to the forecasted schedule of a project at its outset will impact when the depreciation will start. Any variance from the project schedule used to align a project's depreciation schedule in the CIF, including while the project is in implementation, will impact the money used to fund capital investments. From 2010 onward, DND's dedicated accrual budget for capital investments has been almost continually adjusted, to "reprofile" the funds into the future. While some projects have moved faster than expected, such as the Armoured Combat Support Vehicle, overall the reprofiling has been the result of delays to procurement projects, which have meant both that money has not been spent as fast as originally envisioned on a cash basis (detailed below) and that the acceptance of the intended capital asset has been delayed, thereby requiring a reprofiling of the CIF. Unlike other aspects of defence spending which are subject to rules on how much funding can be carried forward from one year to the next, DND is able to reprofile its funds into the future without limit. This provides significant flexibility to align the availability of funding to when it is actually needed. However, the mechanics of the CIF leave funds reprofiled into the future, subject to the impacts of both consumer and defence specific inflation, thereby eroding the purchasing power of defence projects that face delays.[7]

The Implementation of SSE

The implementation of SSE from a spending perspective has several trends. First, as Fig. 1 shows, spending since 2017 has tracked in line with the projection outlined in SSE (the orange line), with the blue line showing actual spending to date, and the dots depicting estimated spending.

However, as Fig. 2 shows, a second trend is that spending on capital has lagged well below the projection contained in the policy. In the three years immediately after SSE was published, DND reversed the trend of leaving significant amounts of its allocation un-spent at year's end, reducing the un-spent allocation of capital to roughly a couple hundred million dollars annually. That situation started to change in 2020/2021, when DND left un-spent $855 million of its allocation, followed by $1.146 billion in 2021/2022.[8] These amounts represent 15% and 20%

Fig. 1 Data reflects total ministry spending, or estimated spending, on a cash basis. Public Accounts, Vol. 2 various years, Supplementary Estimates C, 2022/2023, Main Estimates 2023/2024, and projected spending from Strong, Secure, Engaged, converted to $2023/2024 Billions by the author using DND's Economic Models (various years)

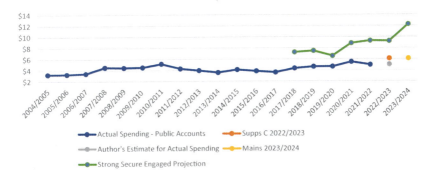

Fig. 2 Data reflects Vote 5 spending, or estimated spending, on a cash basis. Public Accounts, Vol. 2 various years, Supplementary Estimates C, 2022/2023, Main Estimates 2023/2024, and projected spending from Strong, Secure, Engaged provided to the author, converted to $2023/2024 billions by the author using DND's Economic Models (various years)

of the annual allocation, respectively. The underspend in these years was influenced by the economic circumstances created by the COVID-19 pandemic, such as the impact of public health measures on workforce productivity and supply chain disruptions.

Since SSE published a forecast of its Capital spending, it is possible to compare how much of the projected allocation is actually being spent, in other words, comparing the forecast from the policy with actual results. By this metric, DND's underspending is much more pronounced, keeping in mind that *SSE* was predicted on a dramatic, rapid increase in capital expenditures of over 300 percent in inflation adjusted dollars by 2027/2028. By this metric, the shortfall between what DND had envisioned spending in SSE and what it has actually spent ranged from $1.7 billion in 2019/2020 to $4 billion in 2021/2022 since 2017/2018 (see Fig. 2). Based on the total provided in the 2023/2024 Main Estimates, the total by the end of that fiscal year could reach roughly $20 billion over the seven fiscal years since SSE was published.[9] DND's significant and ongoing difficulty spending capital procurement money since 2007 suggests that DND's longstanding problem of having an inadequate supply of capital funds has been supplanted by a structural inability to spend the capital money it has.

The significant shortfall in spending on capital compared to SSE estimates means that a third trend: the significant rebalance of the internal allocation of defence spending envisioned with the policy has not occurred. The spending plans in SSE would have seen capital consuming 34% of defence expenditures by 2021/2022, whereas in fact, the percentage of spending devoted to capital that year was only 16%.[10] The significant increase envisioned in SSE reflected a presumed implementation of the most ambitious capital investment program for DND since the Korean War. However, five years since the publication of SSE, despite progress on several major projects, the major ramp-up in capital investment has yet to occur. According to DND data from December 2021, published by the Parliamentary Budget Officer (PBO), DND's revised plans are for an even more significant increase in capital spending than originally envisioned. As Fig. 3 from a March 2022 report by the PBO shows,[11] the revised forecast of DND spending will see spending rising to an even higher peak than originally planned, reaching $16 billion in 2027/2028, and remaining at a higher level over time than originally envisioned, as of spending plans from December 2021. Given the difficulty experienced thus far, and absence of major procurement reform,

Fig. 3 SSE 20-year cash flow (*Sources* PBO, DND)

Table 1 Canadian defence spending by component ($2021/2022B)

Fiscal Year	2016/2017	2017/2018	2018/2019	2019/2020	2020/2021	2021/2022	% Increase 2021/2022 vs 2016/2017
Capital	$ 3.06	$ 3.69	$ 4.33	$ 3.92	$ 4.67	$ 3.89	27%
O&M	$ 7.74	$ 8.19	$ 8.17	$ 9.14	$ 8.04	$ 8.72	13%
Personnel	$ 10.21	$ 13.39	$ 10.75	$ 10.70	$ 14.94	$ 11.48	12%
Total	$ 21.27	$ 24.91	$ 22.98	$ 24.14	$ 28.20	$ 24.94	17%

Public Accounts of Canada, Vol. 2 converted to $2021/2022 billions using the DND Economic Model by the author.

lagging increase in the capacity of the civilian components of the acquisition workforce, and major shortfall in the CAF's ranks, there is significant room to question whether such an aggressive rate of increase is at all feasible barring either a major increase in acquisition workforce capacity, change to Canada's defence acquisition processes, or both.

Despite the difficulty in meeting the massive capital spending increase contained in SSE, it is notable that spending on defence overall, and capital specifically, has reached a multi-decade high since the publication of SSE, as Figs. 1 and 2 show. Adjusted for Canadian defence specific inflation, in 2020/2021 spending overall, and on capital, exceeded the level reached in 2010/2011 at the height of the war in Afghanistan. Even with a decrease in total real spending between 2020/2021 and 2021/2022 as well as spending on both personnel and capital, as Table 1 shows, in 2021/2022 spending across all three components of the budget and overall all has increased significantly in real terms.

SSE AND BEYOND

Since the publication of SSE, DND has seen its budget increased four times. The 2020 Fall Economic Statement indicated another, significant reprofiling of DND's CIF to align the funding with actual project needs. As has been the case historically, this saw significant shift of funds into the future due to project delays. There was also an adjustment that saw an additional $4.4 billion (on an accrual basis) added to the project budgets of existing SSE projects that had known budget shortfalls. Further, after reprofiling $8.9 billion on an accrual basis out beyond the original SSE twenty year window that ended in 2036/2037, DND was allowed to retain the equivalent value—$8.9 billion—"for anticipated future requirements"[12]—within the original SSE twenty year window. This accounting maneuver allowed defence to align funds in the CIF tied to delayed projects, while also retaining the ability to invest an equivalent sum in other projects, subject to DND bringing forward a new plan for those investments to the Department of Finance. As described below, these funds were used to support NORAD modernization.

In the immense 2021 Budget detailing the ramifications of the COVID-19 pandemic and bevvy of government support programs, DND received a small net budget increase of $1.9 billion over five years, on an accrual basis. The itemization of the budget increase covered defence personnel, operations, and capital investments, as outlined in Table 2.[13] A net $290 million was added to extend Canada's Operation Impact in the Middle East, and $847 million in funding for NATO split between a commitment of an additional six fighters and frigate for a NATO readiness initiatives, as well as increased NATO common funding contributions. A net $77 million was added for a range of responses to the military's culture and conduct crisis as well as $134 million for health services. Lastly, $267 million was added for defence IM/IT systems, and $252 million was included for NORAD modernization divided between $88.8 million to extend the North Warning System and $163.4 million for "seed money" to begin the process of extensive upgrades to NORAD overall.

Budget 2022

Whereas the expectations for significant defence news in the Fall Economic Statement in 2020 and Budget 2021 had been relatively low, expectations for an increase in defence spending ahead of Budget 2022 were higher than any other budget in recent memory. Russia's invasion of Ukraine on February 24, 2022, created an intense interest in defence and security issues and Prime Minister Trudeau left the impression that the invasion had made his government "open to raising Canada's military spending."[14] Speculation ratcheted up even further when the Minister of National Defence stated in an interview that "I personally am bringing forward aggressive options which would see, potentially, exceeding the 2% level, hitting the 2% level, and then below the 2% level."[15] It was unusual language for a Cabinet minister ahead of a budget, but the comments fit with the tenor of discussion from many NATO countries at the time.

The ensuing Budget 2022 delivered a modest increase to defence spending, a promise to review Canada's defence policy and the Trudeau government's first expenditure reduction exercise. Budget 2022 provided

Table 2 Budget 2021 defence measures ($ millions)

	2020-2021	2021-2022	2022-2023	2023-2024	2024-2025	2025-2026	Total
Addressing Sexual Misconduct and Gender-based Violence in the Military	0	64	63	37	37	35	236
Sustaining Health Services for the Canadian Armed Forces	0	26	26	27	27	28	134
Increasing Canada's Contributions to NATO	204	320	320	326	327	334	1831
Extending Canada's Middle East Strategy		527					527
Modernizing DND's Information Systems	0	89	48	60	36	34	267
Supporting NORAD Modernization	0	45	62	54	52	39	252
Less							
Existing DND funds for Sexual Misconduct and Gender	0	-30	-30	-33	-34	-32	-159
Existing DND funds for NATO	-153	-153	-153	-153	-153	-217	-984
Existing Funds for Middle East		-237					-237
					Total Increase		3247
					Existing Funds		-1380
					Net Increase		**1867**

an overall increase of $8 billion (on an accrual basis) over 5 years to "strengthen Canada's contributions to our core alliances, bolster the capabilities of the Canadian Armed Forces; continue to support culture change and a safe and healthy working environment in the Canadian Armed Forces and reinforce Canada's cyber security."[16] Beyond this, according to data provided by finance officials, elaborating on the budget's Chart 5.1 which outlined forecasted funding for DND through 2026/2027 on a cash basis, the additional funding provided in Budget 2022 would result in an annual increase in spending of 3% in 2022/2023[17] rising to 8% by 2026/2027. With consumer inflation running at a multi-decade high, and many commodities critical to defence production experiencing dramatic cost increases, it is unclear how significant an annual increase the spending will produce once defence specific inflation is factored in. According to a senior government official in the budget lockup, if the anticipated defence spending occurs as forecast and the budget's other assumptions hold, by the end of the Budget's fiscal period, defence spending would reach approximately 1.5% of GDP.[18] The Budget itself though makes no mention of defence spending as a share of GDP, so this should not be construed as a spending target.

A full itemization of that $8 billion is provided in Table 3. The main areas of spending are: "Reinforcing our Defence Priorities;" "Supporting Culture Change in the Canadian Armed Forces;" "Enhancing Canada's Cyber Security;" "Supporting Ukraine;" and the "Renewal of Operation Artemis." Working through that list in reverse order, the extension of Operation Artemis, a counter terrorism, and maritime security mission in the Middle East was renewed in August 2021 and will cost of $120 million over three years. The defence portion of the support for Ukraine contains two major initiatives. The first is an extension of Operation Unifier ($338 million from 2022/2023 to 2024/2025) Canada's military support mission for Ukraine, which has evolved from a focus on training Ukrainian forces to a broader set of activities supporting Ukraine's fight. The second component of the support to Ukraine is $500 million in 2022/2023 to provide additional military aid to Ukraine. This money will flow through DND, but be used to actually obtain additional military supplies and provide it to Ukrainian forces. These commitments included additional electro optical systems for Ukrainian drones and culminated with the announcement that Canada would send 39 Armored Combat Support Vehicles, originally purchased for the Canadian Army, to Ukraine.[19]

THE DEFENCE BUDGET 123

Table 3 Millions, accrual basis

	2021/2022	2022/2023	2023/2024	2024/2025	2025/2026	2026/2027	Total
Reinforcing our National Defence							
Reinforcing our Defence Priorities		$ 100	$ 1,025	$ 1,475	$ 1,625	$ 1,875	$ 6,100
Supporting Culture Change	$ 1	$ 38	$ 49	$ 52	$ 53	$ 53	$ 245
Less Departmental Resources	$ (2)	$ (1)					$ (3)
Less reallocation of funding	$ 1	$ (1)					
Enhancing Canada's Cyber Security Addressing the Cyber Threat Landscape	$ -	$ 88	$ 128	$ 187	$ 223	$ 249	$ 875
Enhancing Canada's Cyber Security Research	$ -	$ 1	$ 1	$ 4	$ 6	$ 6	$ 18
Supporting Ukraine							
Expansion of Operation Unifier	$ -	$ 116	$ 112	$ 109			$ 338
Less existing Funds		$ (5)	$ (2)	$ (2)			$ (9)
Bolstering Ukraine's Fight		$ 500					$ 500
Renewal of Operation Artemis	$ 37	$ 43	$ 39	$ 2			$ 120
TOTAL							$ 8,184

On the cyber front, several initiatives were announced, totaling $875.2 million from 2022/2023 to 2026/2027 to enhance Canada's cyber defences, and $17.7 million over the same time period to establish a cyber research chair program. The enhancements to cyber defences include the ability of the Communications Security Establishment (CSE) to launch cyber operations to prevent and defend against cyber-attacks ($263.9 million); improvements to CSE's ability to prevent and respond to cyber-attacks on critical infrastructure ($180.3 million); funding for CSE to make critical government systems more resilient ($252.3 million); and an expansion of cyber security protections for small departments, agencies and Crown corporations ($178.7 million). Supports to Culture Change in the Canadian Armed Forces include $144.3 million over five years to expand health services and physical fitness to be "more responsive to women and gender-diverse military personnel" and $100.5 million over six years for a range of initiatives including strengthening leadership in the Canadian Armed Force; modernizing the military justice system; and engagement and consultation on culture change.

Finally, the most significant funding line in the Budget for Defence was $6.1B over five years, starting in 2022/2023, for "defence priorities, including our continental defence, commitments to our allies and for investments in equipment and technology to immediately increase the capabilities of the Canadian Armed Forces."[20] Roughly half of this was subsequently identified as funding for continental defence modernization, discussed further below.

Looking forward, the Budget also committed to two potentially consequential measures for defence. The first is the Trudeau government's second defence policy review, which will cover "amongst other things, the size and capabilities of the Canadian Armed Forces, its roles and responsibilities, and making sure it has the resources required to keep Canadians safe and contribute to operations around the world."[21] In her Budget Speech, finance minister Chrystia Freeland stated it would be "a swift defence policy review to equip Canada for a world that has become more dangerous."[22] A senior official in the budget lockup indicated that the review would be broad and examine the level of funding required to support the full array of Canadian defence commitments.[23]

Finally, the 2022 Budget indicated that the Trudeau government has entered into what it describes as a period of more restrained fiscal policy. The Budget announced a review of previously announced spending with the objective of reducing the pace and scale of spending that has not yet occurred by up to $3 billion over the next four years. It is also launched a comprehensive Strategic Policy Review, targeting $6 billion over five years, and aimed at $3 billion annually ongoing. No details were provided about the impact to any particular area of government, but during the last round of expenditure restraint during the 2010s, DND contributed about one-fifth of the overall savings, proportional to DND's share of government operating expenses.

NORAD Modernization: Trudeau's Defence Policy, Part 2

On June 2022, the Minister of National Defence presented the Government of Canada's plan for NORAD Modernization. This announcement came after a couple years of active efforts by the Department of National Defence and Canadian Armed Forces, especially senior officers assigned to NORAD, discussing *continental defence* modernization, and the imperative created by renewed great power competition to improve the defence of North America against a wide array of threats.

The NORAD Modernization announcement pledged investments in five areas: surveillance systems; command and control; advanced air to air missiles; infrastructure and support capabilities; and science and technology investments.[24] In discussing these investments, the Minister of National Defence highlighted $4.9 billion in spending over six years, and indicated that the plan was funded for the long term, with a total value of approximately $40 billion over twenty years. When asked if the $4.9 billion was new funding, the Minister of National Defence indicated that it was and that it was on top of funding provided in Budget 2022.[25]

An explanatory backgrounder quietly issued two days later, and unavailable to the media covering the announcement itself, clarified that the figure of $4.9 billion figure cited by the minister referred to funds set aside on a cash basis (the amount over six years is $3 billion) and that the funding had been allocated in Budget 2022. This essentially suggests that the Minister misspoke during the announcement and conflated accounting formats when describing the funding over various time frames. A week after the announcement, when asked if the $4.9 billion the Minister had mentioned was new money, or was being reallocated from existing funds within the department, the Chief of Defence Staff (CDS) replied: "I haven't completely figured out myself the sources of funds for this."[26]

The need for clarification, then the unusual comments about a lack of certainty from the CDS, on top of the initial announcement which was organized on short notice, without American involvement (strange for a major announcement about a binational CAN-US defence arrangement), coalesced to create significant uncertainty about the funding for NORAD Modernization. Several attentive observers have questioned whether there is actually any new funding assigned to the initiatives at all or whether it is rather "pretend money" as one prominent Canadian defence academic called it.[27]

A month after the announcement DND published a fact sheet further clarifying the financial underpinnings of the NORAD modernization initiative. That document indicates that "The incremental funding for the first six years of NORAD modernization comes from existing, previously announced funding. Planning for NORAD modernization has been underway for several years, and the Government of Canada previously announced funding for elements of continental defence and NORAD modernization in Budget 2022, as well as defence funding in Fall Economic Statement 2020" and "The most recent NORAD modernization announcement provides new funding beginning after year six."[28]

Parsing the NORAD modernization fact sheet, with the aid of conversations with defence officials, the funding for NORAD modernization (on an accrual basis) appears to contain the following sources of funds. The first is Budget 2022, which highlighted $6.1B over five years of accrual funding, but did not specify how much money was provided to DND over a twenty year time period. In fact, Budget 2022 provided $12.2 Billion, on an accrual basis, toward NORAD modernization. Since the budget was published in April, at the time of the June announcement, this funding had already been provided to DND. A second source of funds was the "$8.9 billion for anticipated future requirements," previously discussed that had been announced in the 2020 Fall Economic Statement, on the condition that DND returns to the Department of Finance with a plan to spend the money. NORAD modernization provided the funding decision about how that money will be used. Third, and finally, new funding of roughly $17.5 Billion, not previously in the fiscal framework, was provided with the NORAD modernization announcement itself. Added all up, that amounts to the total of $38.6 billion, on an accrual basis, announced by the minister. With such a complicated combination of funding sources, it is not hard to comprehend how it may have been difficult to understand, or communicate, the fiscal aspects of the announcement.

The fact sheet published after the announcement also itemized the funding across a number of capability investment areas, which is presented in Table 4. These break down along five major themes. First, domain awareness will be enhanced through two Over the Horizon radars and additional classified sensors. Second, command, control, and communications will be improved through a modernized Combined Air Operations Center, satellite and radio communications, and other measures. Third, existing stocks of short and medium range air to air missiles will be increased and new long range air to air missiles purchased. Fourth, northern presence will be enhanced by acquiring additional multi-role tanker aircraft, over and above the existing project, and virtually all of the infrastructure supporting Canada's fighter fleets will be upgraded. Lastly, a significant research and development effort is being funded through Defence Research and Development Canada.

DND's Chief Financial Officer stated at a Canadian Global Affairs Institute conference that the total cash value of NORAD modernization is $87 billion over twenty years. For the sake of comparison, she noted that SSE contained $53 billion in new cash funding over an equivalent time period, making NORAD modernization a more substantive undertaking, at least from a capital investment perspective. As notable as the significant size of the new spending, roughly $50 billion over twenty years will be devoted to the infrastructure enhancement itemized in the fact sheet.

While historical data is difficult to come by, this likely makes NORAD modernization one of the single largest upgrades to the DND real property portfolio ever and places the magnitude of the planned infrastructure investments on par with those for equipment. It is entirely unclear if DND has the capacity to invest such a sum, so quickly, especially given the unique circumstances of much of the work. Many of the key locations for upgrading are located in the austere, remote, and infrastructure poor Canadian Arctic and will be subject to country wide labor pressures in the construction industry and worsening demographics in the skilled trades. Further, much of the work will be subject to unique contracting considerations arising from the Government of Canada's obligation to award aspects of federal contracting to Inuit firms under the provisions of the Nunavut Territorial Agreement.[29] All of these factors will increase the complexity of the work envisioned, creating the distinct possibility that DND may be extending its difficulty spending its capital funds to include the infrastructure side of the capital portfolio.

Table 4 NORAD modernization investments (billions, accrual basis)

Funding	Area of Investment	Individual Investments
$6.96	Bolstering our ability to detect threats earlier and more precisely by modernizing our surveillance systems.	Arctic Over-the-Horizon Radar
		Polar Over-the-Horizon Radar
		Classified Sensors
$4.13	Improving our ability to understand and communicate threats to decision-makers in a timely manner through investments in modern technology.	Modernize command, control and communications capabilities
		modernize the Canadian Combined Air Operations Center
		Renew the CAF's high and low frequency radio capability
		Enhance satellite Communications in the Arctic
		Procure new digital radios
		Expand support for the Pathfinder program
		New Positioning, Navigation and Timing capability
$6.38	Strengthening our ability to deter and defeat aerospace threats by modernizing our air weapons systems.	Short range air to air missiles
		medium range air to air missiles
		long range air to air missiles
$15.68	Ensuring our Canadian Armed Forces can launch and sustain a strong military presence across the country, including in Canada's North, through investments in new infrastructure and support capabilities.	Acquiring additional air to air refueling aircraft
		upgrading infrastructure at four locations in Canada's north
		Upgrade fighter infrastructure across Canada
		Modernize air operational training infrastructure
$4.23	bilities to defend North America through investments in	DRDC Science and technology program to assess new threats
$1.18	Internal Services	
$38.56		

Budget 2023

The March 2023 budget came and went without providing any funding to support the review of defence policy announced in Budget 2022 and described above. Given the template established by the Trudeau government for SSE, where the policy was published without the preceding budget providing any funding to support it, this is not entirely unexpected. The budget did outline initiatives to restrain government spending, however, with measures focusing on reducing eligible spending by 3% a year by 2026/2027, and a 15% reduction in spending on travel and services contracting. At the time of writing, the final details of these measures and their impact on DND were not available, and language in the budget document indicated that some attempts would be made to exempt some portion of defence spending, including that focused on the Canadian Armed Forces, specifically, from the reductions. Given that DND represents no less than a fifth of the total pool of each of the spending categories slated for reduction, however, it is difficult to think that much defence spending can be exempted if the government actually intends to produce meaningful spending reductions. Depending on how these reductions are applied, the impact to DND could be around $1 billion a year once fully implemented, primarily impacting spending falling under the O&M budget category.[30]

Conclusion

The five years since SSE was published have demonstrated that Canada's key defence funding issue over the near term is the ability to spend the funds available, rather than the adequacy of the overall defence budget. While budget pressures exist in various places, in the aggregate the DND/CAF has had more money than it can spend for years, and this looks likely to be the case given the increases to the defence budget that have occurred since SSE was published. Baring a significant change to the human capacity of the defence team and consequential change to reform Canadian defence procurement to facilitate a significant increase in additional spending, neither of which are apparent at the time of writing, this situation will likely persist. These dynamics will undoubtedly complicate the Defence Policy Update underway in the spring of 2023. While it is likely the case that the DND/CAF feels there is a large financial shortfall between the existing defence budget and how much the organization believes is required to deliver on Canada's defence commitments, the inability to spend existing approved funding and deliver extant policy will probably complicate the discussions about future increase to the defence budget to support the revised policy.

Notes

1. Government of Canada (2017a, p. 59).
2. Government of Canada (2014).
3. Fetterly (2009).
4. Government of Canada (2017b).
5. Government of Canada (2017a).
6. Rempel and Young (2014)
7. Parliamentary Budget Officer (2022).
8. Government of Canada (2022d).
9. Author's calculations using projected capital spending data for Strong, Secure, Engaged provided to the author, Public Accounts of Canada, Vol. 2 (various years), Supplementary Estimates (C) 2022/2023, and Main Estimates 2023/2024.
10. Perry (2020) and Government of Canada (2005–2022).
11. Parliamentary Budget Officer (2022, p. 7).
12. Government of Canada (2020, p. 134).
13. Government of Canada (2021, pp. 297–299).
14. Walsh (2022).
15. CBC News Network (2022).
16. Government of Canada (2022a, p. 133).
17. The increase for 2022/2023 includes the $500 million for military aid to Ukraine. If this is removed, the increase is roughly 1.5%.
18. This would also include the spending that occurs outside of the Minister of National Defence's portfolio that is included in the NATO accepted definition of defence expenditures. This same point was also made in a pre-budget leak to the CBC's Murray Brewster "Defence Getting Billions of Dollars in New Money from Thursday's Budget: Source," CBC News.ca, April 6, 2022. https://www.cbc.ca/news/politics/defence-department-military-canada-norad-ukraine-nato-1.6410530.
19. Brewster (2022).
20. Government of Canada (2022a, p. 135).
21. Ibid., p. 133.
22. Freeland (2022).
23. Senior Government Official, Media availability, Budget 2022 lock-up. Ottawa: April 7, 2022.
24. Government of Canada (2022b).

25. CPAC (2022).
26. Global News (2022).
27. Conference of Defence Associations Institute (2022).
28. Government of Canada (2022c).
29. Canadian Global Affairs Institute (2022).
30. The author's calculations examining DND spending on Special Objects 2 and 4 in the Public Accounts of Canada, 2022 and Vote 1 and 10 spending in the Main Estimates 2023/2024, Canada, Department of Finance Budget 2023 (Ottawa: 2023), and the author's not for attribution conversations with officials in the Budget 2023 lockup and subsequently.

References

Brewster, Murray. 2022. Trudeau Promises to Arm Ukraine with Modern Military Equipment. CBC News. Available at https://www.cbc.ca/news/politics/nato-arms-canada-1.6506611.

Canadian Global Affairs Institute. 2022. Putting Canadian Procurement on a War Footing. Conference Proceedings.

CBC News Network. 2022. Anita Anand: Power & Politics. March 16.

Conference of Defence Associations Institute. 2022. Canada's Future Submarine Capability: 2030 and Beyond. Force Development Series.

CPAC. 2022. Canada Announces $4.9B Investment for NORAD Modernization. Headline Politics. Available at https://www.cpac.ca/episode?id=e51d1aa0-4699-473b-90bb-7c0bc2fa1f74.

Fetterly, Ross. 2009. Budgeting Within Defence. In *The Public Management of Defence in Canada*, ed. Craig Stone, 53–91. Toronto: Breakout Education Network.

Freeland, Chrystia. 2022. *Budget Speech, Budget 2022*. Ottawa: Department of Finance Canada.

Global News. 2022. Eyre, General Wayne: The West Block. June 26.

Government of Canada. 2014. The Reporting Cycle for Government Expenditures. Available at http://www.tbs-sct.gc.ca/ems-sgd/rc-cr-eng.asp.

Government of Canada. 2020. *Supporting Canadians and Fighting COVID-19: Fall Economic Statement 2020*. Ottawa: Department of Finance Canada.

Government of Canada. 2021. *A Recovery Plan for Jobs, Growth, and Resilience: Budget 2021*. Ottawa: Department of Finance Canada.

Government of Canada. 2022a. *A Plan to Grow Our Economy and Make Life More Affordable: 2022 Budget*. Ottawa: Department of Finance Canada.

Government of Canada. 2022b. *Minister Anand Announces Continental Defence Modernization to Protect Canadians*. Ottawa: Department of National

Defence and the Canadian Armed Forces. Available at: https://www.canada.ca/en/department-national-defence/news/2022/06/minister-anand-announces-continental-defence-modernization-to-protect-canadians.html.

Government of Canada. 2022c. Fact Sheet: Funding for Continental Defence and NORAD Modernization. Available at https://www.canada.ca/en/department-national-defence/services/operations/allies-partners/norad/facesheet-funding-norad-modernization.html.

Government of Canada. 2022d. *Public Accounts of Canada*, vol. 2. Ottawa: Receiver General of Canada.

Government of Canada. 2023a. *Budget 2023*. Ottawa: Department of Finance Canada.

Government of Canada. 2023b. *Main Estimates 2023/2024*. Ottawa: Treasury Board of Canada, Secretariat.

Government of Canada. 2023c. *Supplementary Estimates (C), 2022/2023*. Ottawa: Treasury Board of Canada, Secretariat.

Government of Canada, Department of National Defence. 2017a. Strong, Secure, Engaged: Canada's Defence Policy. Available at https://www.canada.ca/en/department-national-defence/corporate/reports-publications/canada-defence-policy.html/.

Government of Canada, Department of National Defence. 2005–2023. Economic Model, Price Trend Forecast.

Government of Canada, Receiver General of Canada. 2005–2022. Public Accounts of Canada.

Government of Canada, Treasury Board of Canada Secretariat. 2017b. Directive on Accounting Standards: GC 3150 Tangible Capital Assets. Available at https://www.tbs-sct.gc.ca/pol/doc-eng.aspx?id=32518.

Parliamentary Budget Officer. 2022. Planned Capital Spending Under Strong, Secure, Engaged—Canada's Defence Policy: 2022 Update. Available at https://distribution-a617274656661637473.pbo-dpb.ca/c7a9b6d526158fb08858faa6012bbe61777939997eb35e4fd6c510e843f21dc1.

Perry, David. 2020. Canadian Defence Budgeting. In *Canadian Defence Policy in Theory and Practice*, ed. Thomas Juneau, Philippe Lagassé, and Srdjan Vucetic, 63–80. London: Palgrave Macmillan.

Rempel, Mark, and Chad Young. 2014. *Scientific Letter: The PORTFOLIO CREATION MODEL Developed for the Capital Investment Program Plan Review (CIPPR)*. DRDC-RDDC-2014-L256. Ottawa: Defence Research and Development Canada.

Walsh, Marieke. 2022. Prime Minister Justin Trudeau Open to Raising Canada's Military Spending. *The Globe and Mail*. Available at https://www.theglobeandmail.com/politics/article-prime-minister-justin-trudeau-defends-canadas-military-spending-below/.

Defence Policy and Procurement Costs: The Case for Pessimism Bias

Philippe Lagassé

Canadian defence procurement is slow, complicated, and understaffed. Although the Canadian government acquires new and updated capabilities for the Canadian Armed Forces (CAF) on a regular basis, there is no doubt that the procurement process is cumbersome and in need of improvement. The Department of National Defence (DND) lacks the capacity to effectively implement the capital programme outlined in Canada's 2017 defence policy, *Strong, Secure, Engaged* (SSE), which explains why funds that have been budgeted for the acquisition of new equipment continue to lapse. At the same time, a number of projects have been underfunded and have had to wait for new money to move ahead. Still other projects, such as the Canadian Army pistol, were apparently delayed by concerns that their requirements unfairly excluded certain competitors.[1] Notwithstanding these issues, however, the Canadian government has advanced large-scale procurements, such as the Canadian Surface Combatant and the Future Fighter Capability Project.

P. Lagassé (✉)
Norman Paterson School of International Affairs, Carleton University, Ottawa, ON, Canada
e-mail: Philippe.lagasse@carleton.ca

© The Author(s), under exclusive license to Springer Nature Switzerland AG 2023
T. Juneau and P. Lagassé (eds.), *Canadian Defence Policy in Theory and Practice, Volume 2*, Canada and International Affairs, https://doi.org/10.1007/978-3-031-37542-2_8

Likewise, numerous other acquisitions of various shapes and sizes make their way through the Canadian procurement system without much fanfare or attention. Canadian defence procurement is not set up for success, but nor is it mired by endless failure. As with much of the CAF's legacy equipment, the procurement process trudges along, doing the best it can considering what it is being asked to do.

Much has been written about why Canadian defence procurement struggles. Canada's procurement problems have been blamed on a lack of accountability, improper requirements, and partisan politics.[2] Each of these factors contributes to Canada's defence procurement malaise. In this chapter, however, I will focus on one issue that merits further study: the relationship between project costs and defence policy. When defence policy and capital budgets are misaligned, it negatively impacts what capabilities are acquired, how much will be spent on acquiring them, and what high-level constraints the acquisition must accept. Too often in Canada, the actual costs of a policy objective are either downplayed or approached with an optimism bias that produces delays and less capability down the line.

Aspirational defence policies, I will further argue, can lock ministers, officials, and the military into misunderstandings and misaligned incentives. These, in turn, exacerbate costing challenges and political machinations that undermine the procurement system as a whole. At their worst, aspirational policies can put ministers and the military into a game of 'defence procurement chicken', wherein the government insists a policy objective must be met at a lower cost, and the military pleads that the policy objective cannot be met unless a capability is sufficiently funded and robust. To dampen the negative effects of these aspirational policies, I conclude, we should replace the optimism bias that pervades Canadian defence procurement with a pessimism bias.

I begin the chapter with an overview of defence procurement in theory and practice, with an emphasis on some of the factors that make the reality of acquiring military capabilities complex. Next, I explore how defence policy interacts with procurement costs, and how this relationship complicates military acquisitions. Lastly, I conclude with a discussion of how more pessimistic policy costing is an essential step towards improved procurement.

Defence Policy and Procurement in Theory

Democratic civil-military relations demand that the armed forces be subordinate to the civilian government.[3] In a procurement context, this means that acquisitions must align with the government's defence policy priorities. This does not imply that the civilian authority can acquire whatever it wants, whenever it wants. Democratic civil-military relations are part of a wider system that includes the rule of law, regulatory procedures, and accountability mechanisms that ensure that decisions are made according to prescribed processes. As with all aspects of modern democratic government, decision-makers and officials have only as much discretion as the rules allow. Given the money and stakes involved for government, the military, and private sector firms that supply capabilities, defence procurement tends to have particularly stringent rules and fairly narrow degrees of discretion.[4]

In Canada, the Prime Minister and Cabinet decide what the military is expected to do, and the armed forces and civilian bureaucracy endeavour to provide the CAF with capabilities to meet the government's objectives. While the Prime Minister and Cabinet have the discretion to determine the government's defence policy goals, the processes and procedures that must be followed to acquire capabilities are highly regulated to guard against corruption, political favouritism, and other forms of improper interference. These processes and procedures further ensure that the CAF and bureaucracy acquire capabilities that accord with the government's policy objectives. The military may prefer certain capabilities, but democratic civil-military relations demand that they only acquire what they require to meet government policy.

With this context in mind, we can turn to how policy is supposed to be translated into capability through the procurement system. Defence policy can outline broad missions that the armed forces are expected to perform. Defending Canada against conventional threats would count as one of these missions. Contributing to collective defence through the North Atlantic Treaty Organization is another example. Defence policy can also provide more direct guidance. It can authorize the acquisition, upgrading, or development of certain capabilities. For instance, Canadian defence policy provided for the acquisition of fifteen modern warships under the Canadian Surface Combatant project.[5] As well, government policy can determine how certain capabilities are acquired. Thus, the Canadian Surface Combatant procurement was required to take place under the auspices of the National Shipbuilding Strategy (NSS). Between these broad missions and specific directives, defence policy can further outline general intents, such as the need to modernize land capabilities or an ability to undertake concurrent operations.

Once the government has outlined its defence policies, they will be translated into particular procurement programmes and projects. These programmes and projects will then be sequenced and sorted by urgency and complexity. An overarching capital programme can then be laid out. In an ideal situation, this capital programme will be carefully costed, then the government will be presented with a funding request. If the request is above what the government is willing to spend, it should adjust its policies, reducing the expectations placed on the military in terms of missions and objectives. Once defence policy and the defence budget have been properly aligned, procurement officials begin implementing the sequenced capital programme.

The next steps in Canada's defence procurement system can be broken down into several phases.[6] Projects identified within the capital programme are approved to begin. These projects then enter options analysis, where their scope and requirements are determined. The cost and feasibility of the project should also be refined during options analysis, and industry engagement should begin during this phase as well. Once a project has completed options analysis and has an approved preliminary statement of requirement, the Department of National Defence (DND) works with Public Services and Procurement Canada (PSPC) and Innovation, Science and Economic Development Canada (ISED) to develop a procurement strategy and the project to enter the definition phase. With further industry engagement, the procurement plan is implemented, usually with a competitive process comprised of a request for bids, an evaluation of bids received, and contract negotiations. Once the procurement details are determined, the departments obtain Treasury Board approval to enter implementation, usually to award a contract and with an updated funding approval.

If all goes well and the procurement delivers as per the contract, the CAF will field a capability that can be traced back to a defence policy mission, objective, or initiative. In theory, this traceability should be clear and both the military and civilian authority should agree that the capability reflects Canada's policy priorities. Unfortunately, the chasm between this theory and the reality of military acquisitions is often wide in Canadian defence procurement.

The Reality of Defence Policy and Procurement

Canada's defence procurement is far more complicated and less linear than formal processes suggest. Of course, this is true for all countries.[7] No state acquires military capabilities in a manner that neatly follows their established timelines and procedures. Similarly, every country has dynamics, some widely shared, others particular to them, that complicate military acquisitions. Before examining how defence policy produces particular challenges, it is worth examining wider structures that complicate a simple, linear acquisition of military capabilities.

Defence procurement projects do not work with a blank slate. There is already a pre-existing military that new capabilities must interact with and build upon. Militaries, moreover, are generally active. They deploy and use the capabilities they currently have. It is not feasible to press pause on the military and its activities while new capabilities are considered and integrated. Defence procurement, then, must work with a force that is in motion and that has established parts and protocols that new capabilities must fit within. To use some analogies, defence procurement is often like trying to upgrade a plane that is already in flight or to renovate a house that is being lived in.

What does this mean in practice? It means that new systems must be able to communicate with legacy ones; it means new aircraft may need to fit into old hangars; it means that new capabilities may need to conform with suboptimal concepts of operations because they must be used alongside legacy systems that will not be replaced for some time. Simply put, procurement projects add to an existing ecosystem. From the outset, therefore, procurement projects are constrained by fixed assets, interdependencies, standard operating procedures, and integration challenges. Importantly, when critics decry that too many Canadian procurements are 'Canadianized', rather than being bought directly 'off the shelf', they may not realize that the new capabilities must be tailored to fit with the force, protocols, and procedures that are already in place.[8]

Decisions about what the armed forces will look like in the future also impose constraints. As much as procurements must build upon what is, they must be equally mindful of what will be. Projects will often be dependent on the delivery of other capabilities. Planners must ensure that future capabilities will be compatible and interoperable. Project teams must coordinate with other officials, such as those charged with infrastructure and information technology, to ensure that new equipment can be properly absorbed. Here, too, there is an inevitable degree of tailoring and sorting that must take place to make sure everything hangs together down the line. Compounding this challenge is allied interoperability within the North Atlantic Treaty Organization (NATO) and among the Five Eyes (Australia, Canada, New Zealand, the United Kingdom, and the United States). Force planners must ensure that future capabilities adhere to allied standards, protocols, and technological developments that underpin military interoperability. For small and mid-sized states who seek to be fully interoperable with the United States, this can be a particularly daunting challenge, since the American military sets the pace of technological change with a procurement budget that vastly exceeds that of any other country.

Most importantly, all defence procurements confront the 'iron triangle' of cost, scope, and time (Fig. 1). Any decision to prioritize one of these three comes at the expense of the other two, and efforts to balance all three mean that none of them will be maximized. The iron triangle has proved particularly troublesome for the CAF. Owing to the small size of the Canadian defence budget and long delays between recapitalizations, the CAF must often try to get the most capability out of a project, while trying to stay within a set budget. This focus on cost and capability means that time has had to be sacrificed in a number of cases, leading many Canadian defence procurements to have long delays. These delays, in turn, exacerbate budgetary challenges, since capabilities cost more the longer they take to acquire. One of Canada's biggest procurement failures, furthermore, can be explained by the iron triangle. The Phoenix pay system project incentivized officials to prioritize cost and time; the government wanted bureaucrats to deliver the new system on time and on budget. Officials did so, but at the expense of a proper scope, as tens of thousands of public servants learned when the system was brought online.[9]

Defence procurements involve significant public spending to provide a public good: military capability to defend the nation and its interests. In most democracies, however, this rationale is not seen as sufficient to justify the expense involved. Politicians understandably believe that defence dollars should benefit citizens and the national economy more directly. Accordingly, defence procurement tends to involve support for domestic industries and/or specific sectors.[10] In the United States, as is well known, defence capability research, development, and acquisitions

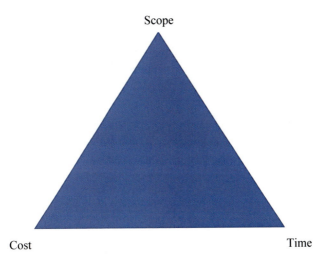

Fig. 1 The iron triangle

maintain a massive American defence industry, which includes both firms that are primarily focused on the military and civilian companies who provide a wider range of goods and services. Canadian defence spending does not allow Canada to have a large defence industrial base, but procurement dollars are still used to support Canadian industry, notably through investments in particular sectors and regions.

The Canadian defence procurement system realizes these investments through the industrial and technical benefits (ITBs) that are assessed as part of bid evaluations.[11] These ITBs inevitably add costs, complexity, and time to the defence procurement process, though the political and economic advantages they provide are too important to abandon. This will also be the case with the federal government commitment to award five per cent of contracts to businesses that are managed or led by Indigenous peoples. One lesson from the COVID-19 pandemic, moreover, would appear to be that states should sustain essential national industries, lest there be a spike in international demand for goods with a limited number of global suppliers. Canada already maintains a national capacity for small arms and ammunition under the Munitions Supply Program, and there may be a need to sustain a comparable domestic capacity in areas such as cyber. Under the NSS, furthermore, Canada decided to rebuild and sustain the country's ability to construct and maintain military and coastguard vessels. The strategy has ensured that there is bipartisan support and economic returns for shipbuilding programmes that will cost well over $100 billion, though it is likely that the policy has increased the cost, complexity, and time facing the recapitalizations of the Royal Canadian Navy and Canadian Coast Guard.[12]

Because defence procurement involves spending large sums of public money on capabilities that will be used in life-or-death situations, the governance structures that surround military acquisition are heavy. Myriad administrative layers and approval processes exist to make sure that projects are acquiring capabilities in the right way, according to an expansive set of rules and procedures. The multiple boards and panels that oversee defence procurements exist for a reason. They are there to identify problems, make sure things are being done correctly, decide on trade-offs when required, and at the highest levels, provide ministerial approval of sensitive and costly acquisitions. As byzantine and bureaucratic as they are, these layers of oversight provide necessary guardrails and can alert officials and ministers to difficult decisions that must be made. When governments are faced with a significant procurement failure or controversy, they have understandably reacted by adding more governance and oversight.

Unfortunately, heavy governance structures also add cost, complexity, and time to already expensive, complicated, and lengthy processes. These structures do not respond well to innovation and they invariably stifle agility. Governance structures that manage and mitigate risks tend to discourage novel approaches and creative solutions.[13] Indeed, risk aversion pervades the entire procurement process, which bogs down the system as a whole. As well, the procurement bureaucracy places "rational people in an irrational system", as one senior official once told this author. Although everyone involved in the procurement system is ostensibly aiming to deliver the best capabilities at the best value, bureaucratic politics and conflict are part and parcel of any large governance structure.

Aside from the hurdles they face within government, procurement projects must also contend with various challenges posed by suppliers. Firms who believe that project requirements are skewed against them can raise objections and potentially force the government to re-assess. While these concerns may be legitimate, they can cause significant delays, and in some cases not have any effect on the eventual outcome of a competition. Large international manufacturers with deep pockets, moreover, can sow doubt about their competitors' products. Too often, a clever ad campaign will gain traction with influential academics and pundits, providing a biased perspective with a halo of purportedly objective, critical analysis. In some cases, the Canadian procurement they are targeting may not even be their primary concern. A Canadian project may be a proxy in a competition for wider markets and buyers elsewhere. Still more problems—many more, in fact—can arise after a contract has been awarded, as the maritime helicopter project highlights.[14] Just because a firm wins a contract, it does not mean that it will be able to deliver on time or on budget; in fact, some contracts are won because a firm has been too optimistic about what it can deliver and for how much.

The reality of defence procurement, then, involves complicating factors that can impede a straightforward delivery of a capability to fulfil policy objectives. While these factors, and many others that have not been highlighted, exist regardless of what policies are being pursued, policy can aggravate them when there is a misalignment with the procurement budget, as we will now discuss.

POLICY AND PROCUREMENT COSTING

Based on how defence procurement works in reality, we can see ways that policy shapes the capability acquisition process. It is government policy, for example, that determines what capabilities must be built in Canada. As discussed, the NSS is one such policy. Similarly, ITBs are a creature of government policy. This is not to say that ITBs are bad policy; they exist for a reason and can be justified on a number of levels. But they are born of policy, nonetheless. The administrative structures that surround defence procurement reflect policy decisions as well. For example, in 2015 the government decided to establish an oversight mechanism, the Independent Review Panel for Defence Acquisition, which this author served on from 2015 to 2022, to provide the Minister of National Defence with a third-party assessment of capability requirements. The lack of new policy direction from the government matters, too. Certain ways of doing things, such as military search and rescue, are a function of *not* reconsidering the location of certain Canadian Forces bases. NATO provides another example. As long as Canada remains in NATO, the CAF is expected to adhere to certain standards and protocols. Each of these represents a way in which government policy, broadly understood, can add complexity to defence procurement, no matter how wise or well-intentioned the policy may be.

To see how the relationship between government decisions and capital equipment budgets can have more detrimental effects, it is important to place the relationship between policy and capability in the context of the iron triangle. As noted, defence policy sets missions and objectives for the armed forces. These missions and objectives determine the scope side of the iron triangle. When Canadian defence policy implies that the CAF must be fully interoperable with allies, for example, this has significant implications for the quality of new capabilities. Full interoperability does not only mean the ability to cooperate on operations. It implies communicating and sharing information and data securely, having systems that can 'speak' to one another, and being able to contribute to a common operating picture and command and control.[15] When the ally with whom Canada wants to interoperate is the United States, the implications are wider still. Achieving full interoperability can involve acquiring capabilities that are controlled by, and only sold with the approval of, the United States. This can limit or prevent competitions for critical capabilities. In addition, interoperable technologies must be regularly updated. This means that Canada needs to keep a constant eye on new technological developments and upgrades to ensure that interoperability does not lag or dissipate.

Another example is the spectrum of conflict. If Canadian defence policy provides that the CAF must be prepared to engage in peer-to-peer conflicts, then the scope side of the iron triangle will reflect adversary capabilities now and in the future. Those charged with translating policy intent into military capabilities will seek to ensure that the CAF has an operational advantage over potential adversaries. As with interoperability, maintaining an operational advantage in the current, highly dynamic technological environment means consistent updates. Maintaining an operational advantage, furthermore, can tip the balance of the iron triangle quite heavily on the side of quality, while placing significant pressure on cost and time to keep up with the latest innovations.

The intimate relationship between defence policy objectives and the scope side of the iron triangle can exacerbate two sets of problems. Above all, it is important to appreciate that ministers may not understand the implications of their policy preferences. Ministers may not be aware, for instance, that full interoperability with the United States can only be achieved in certain ways, with specific capabilities. They may not appreciate that having the CAF be able to fight along the full spectrum of conflict requires keeping the Canadian military constantly ahead of potential adversaries. As importantly, even if they understand the implication for one set of capabilities, they may not appreciate what this means for the wider CAF, given inter-dependencies between various systems and the need to maintain a joint force that can operate in a unified manner. And if ministers are not always cognizant of what their policies imply, opposition critics, pundits, and suppliers will be less able to understand, not having the same access to defence officials who can explain the details and ramifications. This lack of information can be particularly consequential when critics question the need or requirements for certain capabilities. To be blunt, it is incredibly easy to cast doubts on project requirements or question whether they must be met in a certain way or at a particular threshold. These doubts, moreover, will tend to be echoed by skeptical journalists and smug academics who are always on the lookout for failings or shortfalls that fit their particular narratives about the failure of Canadian defence procurement (this author says this as one of these smug academics). The lengthy effort to replace the CF-18 fighter aircraft illustrates how this lack of understanding can create significant problems for Canadian defence procurement. Any doubt that could be raised about this project was raised, multiple times, over more than a decade, causing successive governments to approach the file with a great deal of caution and hesitation.

Costing is the second and main problem. As the concept of the iron triangle emphasizes, when funding is limited, it is necessary to sacrifice the project's scope to stay within budget. Unfortunately, if defence policy demands a particular level of capability to achieve its missions or objectives, planners will be in a bind. Either they must seek additional funding to meet government policy or they must fall short of properly meeting the policy. Understandably, defence planners will tend to gravitate towards the former rather than the latter. The government, after all, wants the CAF to achieve particular objectives and missions; it follows that ministers should be prepared to allocate the funding necessary to do so. Yet, ministers may not be inclined to provide additional funding, let alone understand why they should. While the defence minister may be supportive of additional money, the finance minister and ministers with other spending priorities may be less enthusiastic. When this disjuncture between funding and capabilities occurs across several projects, the capital programme will suffer delays as officials try to stretch their budget.

To understand how this problem arises, it is important to go back to how defence policy and procurement interact, and the perverse incentives involved. Ideally, a defence policy should be fully costed and able to adapt when budgets are insufficient, which they almost always are in defence. The government should not set defence objectives that it is unwilling to pay for. But the temptation to outline ambitious policies is strong. Ministers, after all, are concerned with showing off their government's vision for the next few years. In that time horizon, they have an incentive to lay out big ideas and big plans. The armed forces, on the other hand, are concerned with the longer term. They are looking at the capabilities the military needs decades in the future. Military leaders are therefore welcoming of ambitious policies because it gives them the best chance of acquiring what they believe the CAF needs in the coming decades. At this stage, what matters is that there is a defence policy 'hook' for the capabilities. Neither ministers, nor the military, have an incentive to ensure conservative costing estimates at this point. Quite the contrary. They both have an incentive to accept optimistic costing for the capital programme. Ministers who want ambitious defence policies are more likely to get approval from their Cabinet colleagues, and from the Prime Minister and finance minister, in particular, if these policies come with a reasonable price tag. Military leaders will support optimistic costing for the same reason. If the costing proves overly optimistic, it can be dealt with further down the line, once projects are well underway and difficult to abandon, particularly if it involves jobs and contracts in Canada. Optimistic funding breeds an optimism bias; somehow DND/CAF will manage to meet government policy with what they have been given because they have to and have been told to.

In the worst cases, misalignments between policy ambition and costs can foster a game of 'defence procurement chicken'. In this game, ministers pretend that they will pay for the policies they have announced, and the military pretends that they can acquire the capabilities to fulfil these policies within the budget allocated. The optimal outcome for both the ministers and the military is to 'swerve', i.e. to admit that more money is needed to achieve the policy objectives. Thankfully, this can occur, as we have seen with the government's commitment to the Canadian Surface Combatant, which was initially costed at $26 billion and is now pegged at over $80 billion at the time of this writing. But having both sides swerve is not guaranteed. During Stephen Harper's government, for example, certain procurements did not move forward when projects went well-above their funding allotment, notably the Joint Support Ships.[16] The military also has various strategies it can use to try to force the government to swerve, including prioritizing secondary assets while shortchanging core capabilities that must be adequately funded to keep the CAF operating. This happens too often for it to be coincidental.

Optimistic costing is not a uniquely Canadian problem. As Flyvbjerg and Gardner have shown, the strategic misrepresentation of costs in order to get approvals is common and one of the causes of why many large-scale projects fail or experience significant delays. They quote a French architect who noted the following about cost estimates: "This is a budget that was made because it could be accepted politically. The real price comes later". Similarly, an American official observed that: "In the world of civic projects, the first budget is really a down payment. If people knew the real cost from the start, nothing would ever be approved". Once a project has started, moreover, the sunk cost fallacy takes hold, meaning that the perceived cost of abandoning or fundamentally rethinking the project weighs strongly in favour of moving forward regardless of affordability concerns. As the American official observed, "Start digging a hole and make it so big, there's no alternative to coming up with the money to fill it".[17] When the hole in question is a capability gap that defence policy has pledged to fill, either new money will need to be found or procurement paralysis will set in.

Canadian defence planners have made a concerted effort to address this problem of optimistic costing.[18] Accrual accounting methods allow capital funding to be managed with greater flexibility. Funding can be moved between projects so that those which need more money can look to others that may have more than enough. A contingency fund has been built into the capital budget to offset the inevitable cost overruns that certain projects will face. Yet, these measures can only do so much. If defence policy and the capital budget are fundamentally misaligned, some capabilities will lack sufficient funding unless there is a consistent injection of new money.

Looking at Canadian defence policy and the defence budget, it is not difficult to see why funding and costing have been persistent problems for procurement. Canadian defence policy has sought to maintain a technologically advanced, multipurpose, combat-capable force that can operate across the spectrum of conflict and prevail against near-peer adversaries as part of an alliance or coalition. It has stressed the importance of working closely with the United States to defend North America and on operations overseas. Interoperability with the United States and NATO has been an underlying aspect of Canadian defence policy over the decades and continues to be. Among many other smaller and medium-sized projects, Canada's current defence policy provides that the Royal Canadian Navy will acquire 15 surface combatants, two joint support ships, and six Arctic Offshore Patrol Ships, while the Royal Canadian Air Force will acquire 88 F-35 fighter aircraft and the Canadian Army is meant to replace its major fleets of vehicles. Canada is supposed to do so while improving the quality of life for military personnel and maintaining a vast defence infrastructure that is spread out across the country, much of which needs urgent replacement.[19]

The Canadian government has pledged billions to pay for all this over the coming decades. As a percentage of gross domestic product (GDP), however, Canadian defence spending will hover between 1 and 1.5%. Although the percentage of GDP is a clumsy figure that is best used to measure relative effort among allies, it can also serve as a measure of whether a country is spending on par with its ambition. Suffice to say, Canada's defence policy ambitions are not on par with its defence spending. Looking at countries of similar size with comparable ambitions, it is evident that Canada is not spending enough to match its policy ambition. Australia's defence policy ambition is comparable to Canada's stated objectives, and it spends approximately 2.5% of GDP on defence. France and the United Kingdom spend about the same as a percentage of GDP as Australia. Given Canada's 1–1.5% of GDP, Canadian defence policy should reflect a level of ambition that is closer to that of New Zealand or Spain. Yet, even these countries are not a good benchmark, since they are significantly smaller than Canada in terms of landmass and they are largely focused on one geographic region (Australasia and Europe, respectively), whereas Canada must focus on the defence of North America and Europe, owing to its treaty obligations. No matter how creative Canada becomes with accounting practices and funding models, the gulf between its defence policy ambitions and defence spending will remain large and hamper procurement efforts, unless the military budget climbs significantly and stays above 2% of GDP for the next several decades. Unfortunately, there is no indication that this will happen.

CONCLUSION

Readers may wonder whether the issue here is simply that Canada needs to spend more on defence, full stop. If Canada is not spending enough to match its defence policy objectives, this is a funding problem, not a policy question. In principle, this is correct. But this conclusion does not get us very far. Analysts and allies have been calling on Canada to spend more on defence for decades. Nonetheless, defence spending has remained stubbornly below what is required to attain Canada's policy ambitions. Canada spends 'just enough' to say that it is doing what it says it will do, and as long as the CAF avoids significant failures, governments have seen no reason to change this approach.[20] As far as Canada's overall defence posture goes, this is an optimal position for governments to hold.

If we are seeking to better understand the challenges that surround Canadian defence procurement, however, we must cast a more critical eye on policy. While inadequate funding is part of the supply side of the problem, policy is the demand side. Problems with the defence procurement system can only be effectively addressed if both the supply and demand sides of the equation are adjusted. More concretely, this must involve a far more conservative approach to costing Canada's defence policies. Indeed, it may be necessary to replace the DND/CAF's pervasive optimism bias with a pessimism bias. Data from the Conservative's *Canada First Defence Strategy* of 2008 and the Liberal's *Strong, Secure, Engaged* of 2017 will be useful here. As the acquisitions make their way through the procurement system, the differences between the initial rough order magnitude cost estimates and the actual funding required should be compared. If a consistent pattern of overly optimistic costing emerges across projects of various types, complexity, and size, or across the capital programme as a whole, future costing models and assumptions should reflect this reality. Officials from the Department of Finance, DND, and the CAF should strive to present option sets to Cabinet that reflect past patterns. Ministers should know how much their policy ambitions will probably cost future governments and generations. If Parliament wishes to make these decisions more transparent, the Parliamentary Budget Officer could be empowered to examine the costing assumptions of future defence policy statements and capital programmes. Given the billions of dollars involved in defence procurement, this should be an essential part of government transparency.

Of course, it is important to recognize that there are few short-term incentives to be more pessimistic when costing defence policies. As long as government continues to invest more when funding falls short, defence ministers and the military will continue to gravitate towards optimistic costing; it is easier to ask for more money over the years than to present Cabinet with a very expensive bill up front. If, however, federal spending becomes sparser and there is a desire to tackle defence procurement problems at the source, then harder conversations around the true costs of Canada's defence policy ambitions will need to take place.

Notes

1. Pugliese (2022).
2. Plamondon (2010), Berkok (2010), Williams (2006) and Nossal (2016).
3. Feaver (2003).
4. Markowski et al. (2010).
5. Department of National Defence (2017b, initiative 29).
6. Department of National Defence (2017a).
7. Markowski et al. (2010).
8. For more on this point, see Choi and Collins (2022).
9. Office of the Auditor General of Canada (2018).
10. Hall et al. (2010).
11. Innovation, Science, and Economic Development Canada (2022).
12. Office of the Auditor General of Canada (2021).
13. Mack (2020, 2022).
14. Sloan (2014, pp. 35–37).
15. Richardson (2020).
16. Brewster (2014).
17. Flyvbjerg and Gardner (2023, pp. 35–37).
18. Department of National Defence (2017b, pp. 43–47).
19. Department of National Defence (2017b).
20. Leuprecht and Sokolsky (2015).

References

Berkok, Ugurhan. 2010. Canadian Defence Procurement. In *Defence Procurement and Industrial Policy: A Small Country Perspective*, ed. Stefan Markowski, Peter Hall, and Robert Wylie, 209–227. London: Routledge.

Brewster, Murry. 2014. *Failed Navy Supply Ship Bid Costs Harper Government up to $8M: Documents*. Canadian Press.

Choi, Timothy, and Jeffrey F. Collins. 2022. *If Only Warships Grew on Trees: The Complexities of Off-the-Shelf Defence Procurement*. Ottawa: Canadian Global Affairs Institute. Available at https://www.cgai.ca/if_only_warships_grew_on_trees.

Feaver, Peter. 2003. *Armed Servants: Agency, Oversight, and Civil-Military Relations*. Cambridge, MA: Harvard University Press.

Flyvbjerg, Bent, and Dan Gardner. 2023. *How to Get Big Things Done: The Surprising Factors That Determine the Fate of Every Project, from Home Renovations to Space Exploration and Everything in Between*. New York: Penguin Random House.

Government of Canada, Department of National Defence. 2017a. Defence Purchases and Upgrades Process. Available at https://www.canada.ca/en/department-national-defence/services/procurement/defence-purchases-and-upgrades-process.html.

Government of Canada, Department of National Defence. 2017b. Strong, Secure, Engaged: Canada's Defence Policy. Available at https://www.canada.ca/en/department-national-defence/corporate/reports-publications/canada-defence-policy.html/.

Government of Canada, Innovation, Science and Economic Development. 2022. Industrial and Technological Benefits. Available at https://ised-isde.canada.ca/site/industrial-technological-benefits/en.

Hall, Peter, Stefan Markowski, and Robert Wylie. 2010. Government Policy: Defence Procurement and Defence Industry. In *Defence Procurement and Industrial Policy: A Small Country Perspective*, ed. Stefan Markowski, Peter Hall, and Robert Wylie. London: Routledge.

Leuprecht, Christian, and Joel J. Sokolsky. 2015. Defense Policy 'Walmart Style': Canadian Lessons in 'Not-So-Grand' Grand Strategy. *Armed Forces and Society* 41 (3): 541–562.

Mack, Ian. 2020. *Complex Project Delivery Capability Matters*. Ottawa: Canadian Global Affairs Institute. Available at https://www.cgai.ca/complex_project_delivery_capability_matters.

Mack, Ian. 2022. *Military Procurement Innovation Now*. Ottawa: Canadian Global Affairs Institute. Available at https://www.cgai.ca/military_procurement_innovation_now.

Markowski, Stefan, Peter Hall, and Robert Wylie, eds. 2010. *Defence Procurement and Industrial Policy: A Small Country Perspective*. London: Routledge.

Nossal, Kim Richard. 2016. *Charlie Foxtrot: Fixing Defence Procurement in Canada*. Toronto: Dundurn.

Office of the Auditor General of Canada. 2018. Report 1—Building and Implementing the Pheonix Pay System. Ottawa: 2018 Spring reports of the Auditor General of Canada to the Parliament of Canada.

Office of the Auditor General of Canada. 2021. Report 2—National Shipbuilding Strategy. Ottawa: 2021 Reports of the Auditor General of Canada to the Parliament of Canada.

Plamondon, Aaron. 2010. *The Politics of Procurement: Military Acquisition in Canada and the Sea King Helicopter*. Vancouver: University of British Columbia Press.

Pugliese, David. 2022. DND Replacement Program for Second World War-Era Pistols Delayed Once Again. *Ottawa Citizen*. Available at https://ottawacitizen.com/news/national/defence-watch/dnd-replacement-program-for-second-world-war-era-pistols-delayed-once-again.

Richardson, William. 2020. One Horse Race? A Study of Interoperability in Canada's Future Fighter Capability Project. M.A. thesis, Carleton University.

Sloan, Elinor. 2014. *Something Has to Give: Why Delays are the New Reality of Canada's Defence Procurement Strategy*. Calgary: Canadian Defence & Foreign Affairs Institute. Available at https://www.cgai.ca/something_has_to_give_why_delays_are_the_new_reality_of_canada_s_defence_procurement_strategy.

Williams, Alan S. 2006. *Reinventing Canadian Defence Procurement: A View from the Inside*. Kingston: Queen's School of Policy Studies. Available at https://www.abebooks.com/9780978169305/Reinventing-Canadian-Defence-Procurement-View-0978169301/plp.

The Making of Defence Policy in Canada

Thomas Juneau and *Vincent Rigby*

Much has been written on various aspects of Canadian defence: on military history, for example, or on budgets, procurement, and participation in wars such as those in the former Yugoslavia and Afghanistan. There is little, however, on the actual making of defence policy, that is, on the process itself. Even the first volume of this series did not have a chapter exclusively focused on the topic, though it did have chapters touching on related aspects such as the link between policy and outcomes and the role of special interests.[1]

One rare—but dated—exception is the chapter on the policy process in National Defence Headquarters by George Bell in a collection edited by David Dewitt and David Leyton-Brown—published in 1995.[2] Douglas Bland's 1997 volume also offers short explanatory sections introducing the context for successive defence policies, covering those of 1947,

---

T. Juneau (✉)
Graduate School of Public and International Affairs, University of Ottawa, Ottawa, ON, Canada
e-mail: Thomas.Juneau@uottawa.ca

V. Rigby
Max Bell School of Public Policy, McGill University, Montreal, QC, Canada

© The Author(s), under exclusive license to Springer Nature Switzerland AG 2023
T. Juneau and P. Lagassé (eds.), *Canadian Defence Policy in Theory and Practice, Volume 2*, Canada and International Affairs,
https://doi.org/10.1007/978-3-031-37542-2_9

1964, 1971, 1987, and 1994.[3] Two chapters in a broader book on Canada's international policies by Brian Tomlin, Norman Hillmer, and Fen Hampson are also relevant, but they mostly focus on the historical evolution of defence policy, with only limited discussion of its making.[4] Several other publications have focused on specific aspects of defence policy, but without truly diving into the granular mechanics of its development. Michael Hartfiel, for example, discussed the adoption of capabilities-based planning between 1993 and 2004, while Philippe Lagassé, in his report on accountability, examined the responsibilities of various actors involved in defence policy.[5] Over the years, there have also been a few biographies and autobiographies providing insight and offering anecdotes about the defence policy-making process. In their account of the decision to deploy the Canadian Forces to Kandahar in 2005, for example, Janice Stein and Eugene Lang discussed the development of the 2005 *Defence Policy Statement* (DPS).[6]

The bottom line is that there is a clear gap in the literature: an analysis of how defence policy is made in Canada, focusing on the role of the main players and their interactions—a detailed "nuts and bolts" account. This is what this chapter proposes: not an analysis of the substance of recent defence policies, but a discussion of their process. It starts by offering two case studies: the 2005 DPS and the 2017 *Strong, Secure, Engaged* (SSE). It follows with a discussion of the main principles that drive defence policy making in Canada.

We chose these two case studies because they are recent, representing two of the three most recent formal policy statements; for reasons of space, we do not include the other recent one, the 2008 *Canada First Defence Strategy* (CFDS). DPS and SSE are also very different, each offering important but distinct lessons. The 2005 DPS is especially interesting because it was released as part of a broader international policy review, which included a chapeau international policy statement as well as four sectoral policies on the "3D + T"—defence, diplomacy, development, and trade. The CFDS and SSE were both produced in isolation; of the two, we chose to focus on SSE because it is more recent, and because it was the outcome of a much more elaborate process.[7]

The 2005 Defence Policy Statement

The 2005 *Defence Policy Statement*, released as part of the *International Policy Statement* entitled "A Role of Pride and Influence in the World", was an attempt to rehabilitate the Canadian Forces after a prolonged period of budget austerity and mission fatigue. It came a decade after the 1994 Defence White Paper, the first full-scale defence policy statement after the end of the Cold War. While the White Paper retained the concept of "combat-capable, multi-purpose forces" to carry out a wide range of operations in a still unstable world, these forces would come in a much leaner form. The military was significantly reduced in number and its budget slashed roughly by a third as part of a major deficit-reduction exercise led by Prime Minister Jean Chrétien's finance minister, Paul Martin. The White Paper also promised that the Government would be more selective in sending the Canadian Forces on operations, but this promise was not kept. Over the next decade, Canada's military was deployed on numerous complex missions overseas (e.g., Somalia, the Balkans, and Afghanistan) and at home (e.g., the 1998 ice storm). The number of operations in which the Canadian Forces participated between 1989 and 2005 tripled compared to the entire Cold War period. Stretched to the limit and faced with a tarnished public image resulting from the Somalia affair, the Canadian Forces experienced "a decade of darkness" after the 1994 White Paper, according to a future Chief of the Defence Staff, Rick Hillier.[8]

Paul Martin became Prime Minister in December 2003 determined to lead the Canadian military back into the light. The government's finances were in better shape (defence budgets had recently begun to increase again, if only modestly, including an $800 million infusion in 2003), the unstable post-9/11 security environment called for a greater international role for the Canadian Forces, and Martin was looking for ways to distance himself from the Chrétien legacy and perhaps even his own role in decimating the defence budget. But he had greater ambitions. He had already discussed with his closest advisors before coming to power the idea of a broader international policy review that would include foreign policy, trade, and development. He had an internationalist bent from his days as Finance Minister and appeared to view the complex and challenging world facing Canada as demanding an integrated, "whole-of-government" response. This type of review had never been tried before in Canada (and has not since) and encountered some initial resistance from a bureaucracy accustomed to siloed reviews. Martin was also in a hurry—there would be no extensive external consultations as there had been in 1994 (and would be again in 2017). The world was changing rapidly, and time was of the essence. Reflecting this sense of urgency, the Government released a National Security Policy in April 2004 focusing on the domestic capabilities required to respond to the evolving global security environment. The government then turned its attention to the international sphere.

Inside the Department of National Defence, the policy group had read the tea leaves even before Martin's arrival as Prime Minister and had begun preliminary work on a new policy statement.[9] This work kicked into high gear once the new Defence Minister, David Pratt, was formally tasked with conducting a defence review in his mandate letter. The policy group began drafting in earnest in the early months of 2004 but received no explicit government direction and effectively operated in a vacuum. In the absence of a clear commitment from the Department of Finance to major new defence spending (indeed, Finance Minister Ralph Goodale would remain skeptical about further money for defence throughout the review given other spending priorities and the need for NDP support in a minority government), the policy group proceeded carefully. It feared that an overly ambitious policy statement would be rejected by Cabinet or never properly funded. Early drafts were, therefore, status quo in nature, with the only major change being a shift in focus to the defence of North America as the Forces' ultimate no-fail mission. As part of this rebalancing, and to make the policy affordable, international deployments would be reduced.

At the same time, the policy-making process was ad hoc and would remain so. No internal governance structure was established, and military input was limited in the early stages. When eventually shown a draft of the statement, the military responded predictably. Both the Chief of the Defence Staff (CDS), Ray Hénault, and the Vice Chief of the Defence Staff, George Macdonald, found it not only middle of the road, but reductionist. Hénault stated bluntly that such a statement would leave him in an untenable position as CDS.

As the 2004 federal election approached, some clarity began to appear. The Liberal election platform called for the Canadian Forces' rejuvenation, including an increase in military spending and the addition of 5,000 members to the regular force and 3,000 to the reserves. After the re-election of the Liberal government in June, reducing it from a strong majority to a minority, the policy group returned to its previous draft and incorporated these new commitments. But the new Defence Minister, Bill Graham, was unimpressed. He sought a bold new vision for the Forces in a post-Cold War world, one that would help make the case for significant new defence spending. What he received instead, he claimed, was "all steak and no sizzle", according to interviewees. He quickly became frustrated with his civilian bureaucrats and began to muse whether the next CDS, who would replace Hénault after his appointment as Chairman of NATO's Military Committee, could provide him with this sizzle.

The arrival of Rick Hillier was a watershed moment. Dynamic and self-confident, and possessing significant operational experience including most recently as commander of the International Security Assistance Force (ISAF) in Afghanistan, Hillier knew what he wanted and how to communicate it to politicians. He impressed Martin and Graham in meetings before he was appointed to his new position with his strategic vision, ambition, and "can do" attitude. He clearly identified the challenges of the new security environment after 9/11, where terrorism, failed and failing states, and the 3-block war—in which the Canadian Forces could be conducting humanitarian, stabilization, and combat operations in a single theater—predominated. And he made a convincing case for a military that was more flexible, interoperable, and integrated. He envisioned new units, new command structures, and new equipment. Here was the ambition both the Prime Minister and the Defence Minister had been looking for.

Although Hillier did not officially become CDS until February 2005, he was quietly inserted into the policy statement drafting process well before with the full endorsement of the Minister. He began meeting with the Policy Group's drafting team, laying out the details of his vision and shaping the document. While the Policy Group retained the pen and crafted the threat assessment and the broad policy contours of the statement, Hillier assumed leadership and managed virtually all interactions with the Defence Minister and the Prime Minister. He was the conductor; the Policy Group was only the orchestra. While broader governance surrounding the drafting process remained absent, Hillier did appoint small military tiger teams to directly support the policy process. All three services were represented on these teams, with the air force and navy representatives doing their best to balance what they viewed as an army-centric vision.

Hillier's significant role in the policy statement has raised serious concerns about civil-military relations. Defence policy advice is the purview of the department's Deputy Minister. Indeed, the preparation of a major policy statement is one of the most important responsibilities of a deputy. The CDS is responsible for the control and administration of the Forces under the *National Defence Act* and provides advice on military capabilities, force structure, operations, and requirements. In the case of the DPS, Hillier effectively assumed both the CDS and Deputy roles with the full support of the Prime Minister, the Minister, and the Deputy Minister at the time, Ward Elcock, all of whom shared the Chief's view that the miliary deserved a more prominent role in the policy-making process. Hillier solemnly believed that military matters should be best left to the military, not "field marshal wannabees" as he later described some senior public servants.[10] After the "decade of darkness", Hillier seemed determined to rebalance the civil-military relationship and re-establish the Forces as masters of their own fate with little reliance on civilian mandarins. This was a drastic departure from convention.

As these machinations played out, the broader process surrounding the *International Policy Statement* unfolded. It quickly became a quagmire. The Department of Foreign Affairs produced multiple drafts of the overview document but none pleased the Government. The Prime Minister became increasingly frustrated with the department, whom he accused of lacking policy capacity and imagination, while the department returned the compliment, complaining that the Prime Minister did not know what he wanted. The government eventually called in a Canadian academic based at Oxford, Jennifer Welsh, to help finalize the overview document, and it stumbled to the finish line. While the review was ostensibly "integrated" across defence, diplomacy, development, and trade, in practice it was anything but. The interdepartmental consultation process was token at best. Deputy Ministers and Assistant Deputy Ministers of the concerned departments occasionally met to discuss progress but no formal governance structure was put in place to ensure coordination or coherence, resulting effectively in four siloed reviews. The role of the Privy Council Office was minimal. As word came that the Prime Minister had high praise and only minor comments for the DPS, Foreign Affairs did begin to incorporate some of its key themes (particularly on failed and failing states) into the overview document.

As Graham had hoped, the DPS helped pave the way for increased funding for the military. In the March 2005 budget, before the Statement even came out, the Government announced an additional $13 billion over five years for defence, the largest increase in two decades. Graham played a critical role in the budget negotiations, recognizing early on that without adequate funding, the policy would flounder. He lobbied the Prime Minister and his senior advisors vigorously, as well as the finance minister. The new VCDS, Vice-Admiral Ron Buck, led the negotiations with the Department of Finance at the officials' level. He pronounced himself satisfied with the final budget figure. As in the policy space, civilians—in this case DND's Assistant Deputy Minister of Finance and Corporate Services—took a back seat.

Shortly thereafter, Cabinet approved the International Policy Statement, which was hardly surprising given the Prime Minister's hands-on approach and the recent Budget announcement. It was published in April 2005. Many commentators singled out the Defence statement for its clearly articulated vision. It captured Gen Hillier's call for "relevant, responsive and effective" Canadian Forces operating in a complex security environment. It was praised for its emphasis on jointness and interoperability; its creation of new formations such as the Standing Contingency Task Force, Mission Specific Task Forces, and the Special Operations Group, and new command structures like Canada Command and Canadian Expeditionary Forces Command (CANADACOM and CEFCOM, not named in the Statement but subsequently established); its announcement of increased regular and reserve force strength; and its blueprint for the acquisition of new equipment (supported by the funding increase in Budget 2005).[11]

But did the DPS stand the test of time? The Conservatives replaced the Liberal government in January 2006 and released the CFDS two years later. The new government was more domestic-focused, especially on the Arctic, which was reflected in their decisions on capital acquisitions, force structure, and infrastructure. Hillier and the new defence minister, Gordon O'Connor, clashed over the attempted shift to domestic operations as well as procurement decisions such as C-17 strategic airlift. There was progress on a few capital projects (e.g., Chinook helicopters and search-and-rescue aircraft replacement), but some of Hillier's flagship acquisitions, such as the mobile gun system and large amphibious assault vessels—the "Big Honking Ship" as he affectionately called it—never came to pass. And while Hillier's emphasis on jointness, flexibility, special forces, and the separation of operational commands from the strategic level endured, many of his structural changes (the Standing Contingency Task Force, Canada Command, the Special Operations Group) did not. The legacy of the DPS is mixed.

Whatever the final verdict on the shelf life of the 2005 statement, a strong case can be made that it stands out in the history of Canadian defence policy making on several fronts. Notably, for the first and last time, a defence policy was part of a broader, whole-of-government international review. While this process may have been integrated in name only, it provides insights for any government that might attempt to replicate it in future. Bureaucrats have since argued vehemently against such a process, many still bearing its scars after nearly two decades, but it could have value if done the right way with the right governance. The 2021 United Kingdom Integrated Review bears witness in this respect.[12]

Breaking with tradition, the CDS, supported by the Government, effectively ran the policy statement process, pushing the deputy minister into the background. The Policy Group was still responsible for drafting the statement but to all intents and purposes reported to the CDS. This was a dangerous precedent that undermined the civilian role in policy making. While the Government believed it had no choice in the circumstances, the pendulum swung back under the next government, when the deputy minister re-emerged as the driving force behind the Canada First Defence Strategy. In an ideal world, the CDS and DM should work hand-in-glove and challenge each other, but lanes must be respected—as the SSE example below successfully illustrates.

The Prime Minister's role in the making of the international policy statement was unprecedented. He was active in its development, engaging senior officials directly, providing written and verbal feedback on drafts, and signing off on the Statement even before it went to Cabinet. This reflected the Prime Minister's personal working style. In the case of the DPS, it proved invaluable. But the same cannot necessarily be said of the overview document led by Foreign Affairs.

The lack of public consultations stands in stark contrast to the 1994 and 2017 reviews. The government, especially after the 2004 election, was focused on the next Budget and speed was paramount. It may have sensed the prevailing public mood, especially support for a rejuvenated military after years of operational over-stretch, but the total absence of any public engagement, including with parliament, was conspicuous. Meaningful consultations with allies were likewise limited.

Finally, the internal process supporting the development of the DPS was thin and ad hoc. There was no integrated "civ-mil" team, no clear single Canadian Forces contact for the Policy Group (beyond the CDS), no external advisory group, no integrated costing mechanism, and no internal policy committee. The makers of the 2017 policy statement may have learned valuable lessons in this respect.

2017: Strong, Secure, Engaged

As the Liberals took power in 2015 after nine years of Conservative government, they sought to distinguish themselves from their predecessors, including on foreign and defence policy. Their campaign platform included promises to return to UN peacekeeping (which, with one notable exception, did not happen), re-establish diplomatic relations with Iran (which also did not happen), cease contributing CF-18s to the coalition against the Islamic State (a promise they fulfilled), not buy the F-35, and give multilateralism what they claimed was its traditional place in Canadian foreign policy. To deflect criticism that they were "soft on defence", the Liberals also committed to increase defence spending as part of a comprehensive review to replace the CFDS, a short document with limited detail.

Overall, the process that led to SSE was robust: civil-military relations were harmonious (or at least as much as they can be), relations between the Department and the Canadian Armed Forces (CAF, as the CF were now known) and the minister's political office were also generally cooperative; the process was undergirded by extensive analytical work; and perhaps most crucially, the process involved detailed costing analysis, much more than in previous policy reviews. In this sense, the SSE process offers valuable positive lessons—in many ways, the reverse of the DPS.

The Policy Group, led by the Assistant Deputy Minister (Policy), or ADM(Pol), is responsible for the development of defence policy advice and overseeing its implementation. It is the lead pen, directly drafting many portions of major policy documents. It also sets the parameters for the work of other groups within DND/CAF which draft specialized sections, including the military, which develops and analyzes military capability options. Overall, it is responsible for translating political direction into a bureaucratic process that results in an achievable policy.

Within the Policy Group, the Policy Planning division, or DGPolPlan, was the overall lead, the coordinator of the process, and the lead pen for

SSE, as well as key documents such as briefing notes to the minister, the Privy Council Office, and the ministerial panel (discussed below). DGPolPlan also acted as the secretariat for the policy committee, the main DND/CAF governance body for the SSE development process. This was a small group comprising the Deputy Minister and the CDS as well as a limited number of senior officials, including the VCDS and the ADM (FinCS). Other senior officials also attended as required.

The VCDS acts as the chief of staff to the CDS and DM. The VCDS portfolio includes the Chief of Force Development (CFD), which coordinates force development activities across the CAF. CFD (headed by a two-star flag officer) has the lead on drafting and analyzing military options, working closely with DGPolPlan. CFD started preliminary work on analyzing military options prior to the 2015 elections, when it realized that all three major parties had committed to a defence policy review. When the process formally started after the Liberals took power in late 2015, CFD was therefore able to hit the ground running.

CFD's first task was to build a comprehensive understanding of the state of the CAF. On this basis, it started work on broad options to replace capabilities, including prioritizing, costing, and scoping them. To do this, CFD created a working group of about 40 individuals, representing relevant units within DND/CAF (known as L1s). They could then reach out to their home organizations to obtain information and validate progress. CFD created eleven placemats, an 11 × 17″ visualization tool, on core capabilities (for the three services, special forces, and joint capabilities such as cyber, space, and intelligence). This provided a comprehensive picture of the state of the CAF and highlighted areas of greatest need, areas of palpable risk, and areas where risk could be managed. From there, CFD asked all capability stakeholders for hard data on issues such as costs of replacements and life-extension for each capability, as well as timelines and gaps if there was no replacement. On this basis, CFD developed five options; it presented them to military leadership, which chose three. This formed the foundation for the military's contribution to SSE.

More than in the case of the DPS, ADM(FinCS) played a major role in the development of SSE. In particular, it secured an external contractor, Deloitte, under a sole-sourced contract to provide an independently validated costing of the policy; Deloitte's methodology was itself validated by two other external firms. This was key to build credibility with the Department of Finance, which has traditionally been skeptical of DND's budgetary requests.

To make this work, ADM(FinCS) systematically required large amounts of data from the military. There was pushback at first, but over time the cooperation in general was strong. Data on capabilities (notably their costs and timelines) were then entered into a "decision engine"—known as Montecarlo—which ran the process and built options. These options could then be adjusted by changing some of the data (e.g., more or less budget; which replacement for which capability; shorter or longer timelines). This system was flexible: it could integrate, for example, different options to replace the F-18s (e.g., with used F-18s or new F-35s); it could then build the cost and personnel options of various choices into the model. Illustrating this flexibility, only days before the final decision on the policy, the government came back to DND/CAF and asked for a less costly option; using this model, the department was able to rapidly reframe the option set at the last minute. Officials interviewed for this chapter readily recognized that hindsight has shown that the exercise underestimated the eventual cost of projects; nevertheless, they insisted that the process was more rigorous than it had been in the past.

The Privy Council Office played a very limited role in shaping SSE's substance; it was focused on ensuring that DND/CAF met deadlines, on supporting Cabinet when SSE was on the agenda (which occurred on a regular basis) and on regularly briefing the Prime Minister. More broadly, another Privy Council Office role was to act as a form of reality check to ensure that DND/CAF officials understood the political constraints, if for example some options were too ambitious. These responsibilities mostly fell under the purview of the National Security Adviser (as the position was then known, before becoming the National Security and Intelligence Adviser in 2018). The Clerk of the Privy Council was only rarely involved, notably on budget matters and in later stages when the policy was getting ready to go to Cabinet for formal approval.

The Prime Minister's Office (PMO) played an important role at the end of the process. PMO decided at that stage to treat SSE like a budget document—which meant that it would review it line by line and approach it seriously. It even reviewed pictures individually, demanding for example that those on the cover include more people and less military kit. It ended up asking for many changes, ranging from small wording details and pictures to larger ones such as the order of chapters. For example, it is PMO that requested that the chapter on people be moved first (instead of, perhaps more logically, the analysis of the international security environment, which moved to chapter four). There was, notably, extensive back and forth between PMO (including Michael Den Tandt, a former journalist with responsibilities on communications and with some expertise on defence matters) and Defence Minister Harjit Sajjan's office. The latter then repeatedly had to go to senior DND/CAF leadership to discuss PMO requests; in many cases, there was pushback. This went on for several weeks. At the very end, the most senior leadership in PMO (Gerald Butts, personal secretary to the Prime Minister, and Katie Telford, Chief of Staff) reviewed the draft, without asking for major changes.

SSE also differed from DPS in terms of the extensive consultations its development involved. The consultations, the largest since at least 1994 for the development of a new defence policy, were premised on four pillars: with the public, experts, an expert panel, and allies. To manage consultations with the public, first, DND hired a private contractor (Ipsos), as the department did not have the necessary resources or expertise. Ipsos received and analyzed submissions from the general public and then synthesized them into a consolidated report. DND also organized a series of roundtables across the country with academics, civil society, and veterans.

Was this useful? The impact of public consultations is difficult to measure. There was often a validation dimension: consultations did not really bring new ideas, but they allowed ADM(Pol) to confirm when it was on the right track. In some instances, the consultations did allow for useful insights to emerge. For example, both public and expert consultations saw many expressions of concern with the state of the reserves and of search and rescue. This was initially surprising for many in DND, but it made sense: that is where many in the public have a closer interaction with the military.

The third element of the consultations was perhaps the most innovative. The ministerial advisory panel included four eminent Canadians: Louise Arbour (a retired Supreme Court justice), Ray Hénault (a former CDS), Bill Graham (a former minister of national defence and foreign affairs), and Margaret Purdy (a former senior public servant). The panel was established initially because Minister Sajjan wanted an independent source of advice; he and his office did not want to be completely reliant on DND/CAF as their only source of information. As such, the Minister insisted that the panel be well resourced and be kept informed. The panel, as a result, was regularly briefed by DND and CAF officials. There was initially skepticism within DND/CAF, but by the end of the process, most senior officials interviewed for this chapter recognized that the panel had been a valuable addition.

A key ingredient to the panel's success is that it included individuals with diverse perspectives: a former CDS with military knowledge, a retired minister who understood the political context, a retired senior bureaucrat who understood how ideas would need to be implemented, and a retired judge with expertise in the law of armed conflict. It made for frequent clashes of views—especially between Graham and Arbour—but overall its work was collegial. That said, the case could be made that it would have been useful to have an industry representative on the panel: even if politically that would possibly have exposed the government, it would have provided a valuable expertise that the four members did not have.

The Panel's impact is, again, difficult to quantify, but several officials interviewed agreed that it was significant. In meetings, the panel posed tough questions to DND/CAF officials, challenged their assumptions and analysis, and provided valuable feedback. When the Panel agreed with the analysis it received, it validated DND/CAF's work; in many other instances, it pushed back. This forced DND/CAF to solidify their analysis; the work they had to do to be ready to present to the Panel was on its own an important incentive. In the words of one interviewee, "given the tremendous brain power on the panel, every time we went to brief them, it forced us to seriously think through our analysis". Minister Sajjan, in a way, also relied on the panel to be his eyes and ears on the process. One interviewee insisted that the minister's office trusted the Department and the Forces; the panel was not evidence of a lack of confidence in their work, but rather was viewed by Sajjan as a complement.

Finally, policy officials in DND held conversations with allies to share lessons learned before and during the process, notably with France, UK, Germany, and the United States. This was useful in several ways, especially since some allies had recently held similar policy development exercises. Conversations with New Zealand on its force development model and its public consultation exercise were especially relevant. The paper DND released as the starting point for public consultations, in particular, was heavily inspired by the New Zealand model. Australia also gave valuable advice on the critical importance of having independent, outside review of the costing of the new policy through the hiring of a consultant (in fact, DND ended up hiring not only the same contractor, but many of the same employees from that company, Deloitte).

One last question is worth pondering when discussing SSE's development: why did the government agree to such an extensive process? Especially when compared to the DPS or CFDS, SSE is unique: the document itself is well over 100 pages, the exercise included detailed costing and consultations, and it was guided by an extensively structured governance. The explanation is, to some extent, political: the new Liberal government wanted to distinguish itself from its predecessor, whose CFDS was a short document and more a shopping list than a true policy. This suggests an important conclusion: politics and political considerations have a significant impact on the content of the policy, naturally, but also—and perhaps less intuitively—on the parameters of the policy development process. Finally, central agencies such as Treasury Board and Finance have long been critical of the CAF for systematically undercounting the costs of major procurement projects and for not being transparent. The SSE process did not resolve these longstanding tensions, but officials interviewed for this chapter insisted that part of the reason for the detailed costing process was to at least try to counter this widespread credibility challenge faced by the military in Ottawa (see the chapter by Lagassé in this volume for more on these challenges).

Defence Policy Making in Canada

It is difficult to offer a broader discussion on the process of defence policy making in Canada: as our two case studies suggest, every instance is different, and sometimes very different. Nevertheless, there are important lessons that can be learned from the successes and failures of the drafting processes for the DPS and SSE, which can be useful for future policy development endeavors.

The differences between DPS and SSE are striking: for the DPS, the forceful personality of Gen Hillier, supported by an engaged Prime Minister and Minister of National Defence at the political level, largely drove the process, while governance structures—committees, consultations, etc.—played a minor role. For SSE, personalities played a much less important role while the governance was much more structured. Does this matter? In many ways, it does. DPS was a creative document with innovative ideas, but the absence of a rigorous internal process may have played a role in some costly or complex proposals either never seeing the light of day (such as the Mobile Gun System or the Standing Contingency Task Force) or being eventually scaled back (CANADACOM and CEFCOM, responsible for domestic and international operations respectively, were eventually fused into the Canadian Joint Operations Command, or CJOC). In SSE's case, the extensive costing exercise provided a more reliable—if still far from ideal—foundation.

The DPS and SSE cases also offer important lessons on civil-military relations in Ottawa. The defence policy process works best when each side respects the other's lane while keeping each other informed. Ideally, the government should provide clear guidance on what it wants to achieve with its military. On that basis, the military provides capability options on how best to achieve these goals, free of policy or political interference within those parameters. In the case of SSE, interviewees all agreed that civil-military cooperation was, overall, strong. There were inevitable tensions, but these are inherent to the process. As one interviewee put it, in the most basic sense, "the DM and CDS were on speaking terms", which historically has not always been the case. Each respected the other's role, while both supported and kept the other informed. This was clearly not the case with the DPS, with Gen Hillier taking control of the process with full political support and the civilian side allowing itself to be marginalized.

The SSE case also illustrates the importance of gaining and keeping buy-in across Ottawa. Throughout the process, the DM, CDS, and Chief of Staff to the minister (respectively John Forster, Gen Jon Vance, and Brian Bohunicky) held regular meetings with important ministers. Of course, such meetings happen in other contexts, but there was an unusually high number as part of the SSE process. In the words of one interviewee, the three told a "well-integrated story", based on their respective portfolios: the Chief of Staff on how SSE supported the government's political agenda; the CDS on the threat environment, the state of military capabilities, and what the available options to move forward implied; and the DM on the administrative framework. Consistent engagement also occurred through regular Cabinet meetings as well as through GTFAD (Global Trends, Foreign Affairs, and Defence), the main deputy minister committee on such matters at the time. The minister's chief of staff also held a series of meetings with Claude Rochette, the assistant deputy minister responsible for finance, and Mike McNair, the PMO official focused on budget issues, to explain the accounting changes operated at DND and the implications of proposals to increase defence funding. McNair was then able to hold discussions with the Department of Finance, the buy-in of which was essential for what ended up being the largest increase in defence spending in decades. This ensured that there were no surprises once the proposal reached Cabinet for final decision. Illustrating the rigor of this engagement, at Cabinet every minister (and their deputy) had a tailored placemat laying out what the policy meant for them—for their riding and their department. This is clearly distinct from the DPS process, in which the pivotal engagement played out at the highest levels between the CDS, the Minister, and the Prime Minister, who signed off on the document before it even went to Cabinet. Interdepartmental consultations certainly occurred at lower levels, including with Finance and other departments directly involved in the IPS process, but these were not as structured or as deliberate as those carried out under SSE.

The overall rigor of the SSE process is also seen through the work that was done, informally, beforehand: both ADM(Pol) and CFD had already conducted significant background research even before the 2015 elections, when it became clear that the three major parties in the coming elections were committing to a policy review if elected. They had also conducted some analysis in the late years under the Conservatives, when the minister at the time, Jason Kenney, had begun work on a "CFDS refresh". Chapter four in SSE, which offers an extensive analysis of the international security environment, provides an illustration. The government did not provide much guidance to the Policy Group on its views on this matter. One team within the Policy Group, the Directorate of Strategic Analysis (DStratA) had started working on a deep analysis of key trends in the international security environment and how they affected DND/CAF in the years before the process of drafting SSE, notably as part of medium-term planning (transition) in 2015 and through the GTFAD committee.[13] When the SSE process was formally launched, DStratA was able to build on this prior effort. In addition, the drafting of ch.4 included extensive consultations with GAC and the intelligence community, notably the Canadian Forces Intelligence Command (CFINTCOM).

This process had broader benefits, allowing for in-depth discussion and reflections within the public service on changes in the international security environment and their implications for Canada. In its final version, chapter four highlighted key themes that, several years later, have survived the test of time reasonably well, such as the growing ambition of Russia and China, the intensifying proliferation of disruptive technologies, and the erosion of the rules-based international order. Again, these are internal discussions that did not occur to the same extent in the drafting of the DPS. At the time, ADM(Pol) did retain the lead on the threat assessment part of the document, though Gen Hillier's arrival certainly sharpened the final language.

An ambitious policy development process requires, in theory, extensive consultation throughout the bureaucracy (and with external stakeholders, such as experts, the private sector, and allies) to make sure that a wide range of views contribute to the process and that information and proposals are validated and challenged. At the same time, successive drafts cannot be extensively circulated to avoid damaging leaks. This is, in practice, a difficult balance to strike. On the one hand, in the case of SSE, there were no leaks. Yet at some points in the process, the tight circle of trusted people meant that crucial voices were not heard, or were heard later than would have been necessary. For example, the assistant deputy minister for infrastructure and environment was not consulted much, especially early on, yet many of the proposed capability decisions had infrastructure implications that were neglected until late in the process. The option of purchasing F-35s, notably, implied the need for major infrastructure works, such as secure facilities in hangars. In the DPS process, intra-departmental consultation was even more strictly limited. The lack of internal governance—for example, a central policy committee that would oversee planning and drafting and ensure coordination across the Forces and the Department—was conspicuous.

In an ideal world, defence policy would be developed on the basis of clear foreign policy guidance; there should be first some kind of foreign policy statement which would then steer the new defence policy. SSE, however, was developed in the absence of an overarching foreign policy review. Even though many officials in DND/CAF would have wanted to have clearer foreign policy guidance to help them draft a new defence policy, it was clear from the start that it would not be forthcoming. There was some frustration in the Policy Group when faced with Global Affairs Canada's inability to provide more guidance. But in the words of one interviewee, "to be fair, it was the minister's fault, not the department's". This raised several challenges: it was difficult, for example, to identify geographic regions that should be a priority for SSE. As a result, ADM(Pol) had to work hard to estimate what the government's foreign policy was. They were able to glean information from official statements, such as speeches from the throne and the most recent budget. They also consulted Global Affairs, notably to validate that their reading of

Canada's foreign policy was accurate; one interviewee described those conversations as "signals checks". In the case of the DPS, one might have thought that the integrated nature of the process, also involving foreign affairs, development, and trade, would have provided clear foreign policy guidance. This never happened. Since the foreign ministry could not deliver a product that met the Prime Minister's wishes, DND/CF, led by Hillier, took it upon itself to produce their own threat assessment which ultimately drove much of the broader IPS process.

Finally, the DPS and SSE experiences raise important questions about the sustainability of the processes set up during their development phase. The SSE process, which included more detailed costing analysis than in previous policy development exercises, established important precedents. The Montecarlo capability engine has since been improved and is sometimes used as part of regular DND/CAF processes, not just for major policy reviews. For example, when the government announced that it would replace the F-18s with F-35s, the department was able to enter the data (number of units purchased, cost, timelines, etc.) into the model to map out the impact over time.

That said, another issue that the SSE process demonstrated is that even a more rigorous policy development governance structure will suffer from limits if it is not followed by an equally rigorous policy implementation process. As several interviewees suggested, this has been an important gap in the actual implementation—which is not the topic of the chapter, the focus of which was its development—of SSE. For its part, the DPS policy-making process provides clear lessons in how *not* to do a defence review. It is for this reason that, nearly two decades later, bureaucrats (and politicians) still look back on the entire IPS process with some antipathy. SSE, while far from perfect or smooth, stands in stark contrast. Deliberate, structured, and well-governed, it avoided many of the pitfalls that plagued the DPS. It may offer important and valuable lessons for many years to come.

Notes

1. See the chapters by Chapnick and Stone and by MacDonald.
2. Bell (1995).
3. Bland (1997).
4. Tomlin et al. (2008).
5. Hartfiel (2010) and Lagassé (2010).
6. Stein and Lang (2007).

7. This chapter is partly based on a dozen interviews the two authors conducted separately in the fall of 2022 and early 2023. All interviewees were promised anonymity; they were serving and retired civilian and military officials from DND/CAF and other departments as well as senior political staffers.
8. Horn and Bentley (2015).
9. One of us, Rigby, was the Director General of Policy Planning in the Policy Group from 2004 to 2006; in this position, he led the policy drafting team for the DPS. The other, Juneau, was a policy officer in the Policy Group at the time but was not involved with the DPS.
10. Brewster (2010).
11. For context, see Welsh (2006).
12. O'Neill (2022).
13. One of us, Juneau, was an analyst in DStratA until 2014 and had a limited involvement in the early stages of this work.

References

Bell, George. 1995. The Policy Process in National Defence Headquarters. In *Canada's International Security Policy*, ed. David Dewitt and David Leyton-Brown, 323–350. Scarborough: Prentice Hall.

Bland, Douglas. 1997. *Canada's National Defence; Volume I: Defence Policy*. Kingston: School of Policy Studies.

Brewster, Murray. 2010. Hillier Slams 'Field Marshall Wannabes' in Memoir. The Canadian Press. Available at https://www.ctvnews.ca/hillier-slams-field-marshal-wannabes-in-memoir-1.561857.

Hartfiel, Michael. 2010. Planning Without Guidance: Canadian Defence Policy and Planning, 1993–2004. *Canadian Public Administration* 53 (3): 323–349.

Horn, Bernd, and Bill Bentley. 2015. *Forced to Change: Crisis and Reform in the Canadian Armed Forces*. Toronto: Dundurn Press.

Lagassé, Philippe. 2010. Accountability for National Defence: Ministerial Responsibility, Military Command and Parliamentary Oversight. Institute for Research on Public Policy. Available at https://irpp.org/research-studies/accountability-for-national-defence/.

O'Neill, Paul. 2022. The UK's Integrated Review at One Year—Fit for Purpose? RUSI Commentary. Available at https://rusi.org/explore-our-research/publications/commentary/uks-integrated-review-one-year-fit-purpose.

Stein, Janice Gross, and Eugene Lang. 2007. *Unexpected War: Canada in Kandahar*. Toronto: Viking.

Tomlin, Brian, Norman Hillmer, and Fen Osler Hampson. 2008. *Canada's International Policies: Agendas, Alternatives, and Politics*. Don Mills: Oxford University Press Canada.

Welsh, Jennifer. 2006. The 2005 International Policy Statement: Leading with Identity? *International Journal* 61 (4): 909–928.

Printed in the United States
by Baker & Taylor Publisher Services